Reader & Editorial Reviews

"I'm thankful for reading Professional Drug Addict. This story takes readers through the ride of a person who performed and achieved social and financial success yet ultimately found humanity and his greatest gifts through his fall. The beauty in Arnel's story is that his journey lies in each of us. When we choose to express and face our shame, we grow and have the capability to give."

—Melanie O'Cain, Deputy Mayor City of Kenmore

"In Leyva's autobiographical debut, he embarks on an unintentional journey into self-discovery that is all at once painful, truthful, and raw. Leyva shows us how he scratched and clawed his way out of that life and recreated himself. This is a book about hope."

— Samantha Lyons, Kitsap County Superior Court Treatment Court Manager

"A raw, riveting, and ultimately redemptive memoir that peels back the layers of addiction, homelessness, and criminal life in the Pacific Northwest. Arnel Castro Leyva doesn't just recount his descent—he maps the way back with unflinching honesty, hard-won insight, and a deeply human voice. Professional Drug Addict is a vital read for anyone who believes in second chances and the power of transformation."

—Reprospace Editorial Reviews™

PROFESSIONAL DRUG ADDICT

Arnel Castro Leyva

Professional Drug Addict, A Memoir of Addiction, Crime, Homelessness, and Redemption
First Edition, © 2025, Arnel Castro Leyva
Book cover image provided by the author.

Paperback ISBN-13: 978-1-952685-98-9

No part of this publication may be reproduced, stored in a retrieval system, or transmitted in any form or by any means—electronic, mechanical, photocopying, recording, or otherwise—without the prior written permission of the publisher, except for brief quotations embodied in critical articles or reviews.

Author's Note on Tone and Intent
This book is a work of nonfiction that blends memoir, social commentary, and cultural critique. Some passages include candid depictions of hardship, poverty, addiction, and crime as experienced or observed by the author. These narratives are presented not to glorify or condone illegal or harmful behavior, but to shed light on the systemic issues and personal struggles that shape human decisions.

The tone of certain sections may be satirical, ironic, or provocative, intended to challenge readers' assumptions and provoke critical thought. Any references to corporations, institutions, or social systems are made in the context of public discourse and are based on the author's perspective, personal experiences, and available information at the time of writing.

Readers are encouraged to approach the text with an open mind and an understanding that the intent is to inform, question, and explore—not to incite or justify actions that break the law or cause harm.

This is a work of nonfiction based on the author's personal experiences. Names of persons and identifying details may have been changed to protect individuals' privacy. The author has recounted events to the best of his memory and understanding; some dialogue, scenes, and timelines have been reconstructed or modified for narrative clarity.

This memoir contains strong language and mature content reflective of the author's lived experience. The views and opinions expressed in this book are those of the author and do not necessarily reflect those of the publisher, editors, or any affiliated organizations. This book also contains references to drug use, criminal activity, and adult situations that may be disturbing to some readers. It is intended for mature audiences only.

All references to brand names, companies, products, institutions, or services—including but not limited to Walmart, Target, Amazon, Uber, LinkedIn, Adobe, Facebook, Craigslist, and others—are used strictly for descriptive, factual, and narrative purposes.

The inclusion of any trademarked names or identifiable brands does not imply endorsement, sponsorship, affiliation, or association with the entities mentioned. All trademarks and registered trademarks are the property of their respective owners.

Any mention of these names is made under the principles of nominative fair use and is protected under applicable laws relating to freedom of expression and nonfiction storytelling. No logos, stylized brand marks, or likenesses are reproduced.

The author and publisher disclaim any intent to defame, disparage, or misrepresent any individual, company, or organization referenced within the text. This work is not intended to provide medical, legal, or therapeutic advice.

Published by Kitsap Publishing
Poulsbo, WA 98370
www.KitsapPublishing.com

Contents

Acknowledgments

Foreword

Introduction

Chapter 1 Girlfriend Experience	1
Chapter 2 The Life	17
Chapter 3 Suburban Underground	36
Chapter 4 Professional Drug Addict	54
Chapter 5 Grand Identity Theft Auto	73
Chapter 6 Sleepless at Wally's	94
Chapter 7 Phase I	119
Chapter 8 Phase II	145
Chapter 9 Phase III	157
Chapter 10 Phase IV	179
Chapter 11 Launch	197
Chapter 12 Epilogue	207

To Danielle

Acknowledgments

To everyone I met on the streets whose names I changed in the first part of this book, our reciprocal exploitation of one other was fundamental to finding my path (and makes a page-turner of a story). I hope every one of you goes beyond merely making your own way and instead can find your path.

To all the police officers who picked me up and put me in jail while I was on the streets, and especially the very last policeman who seemed as if he would have rather let me go but couldn't when he saw my long list of warrants—thank you for doing your job and putting me on my path.

To all the staff at the SCORE Jail, Regional Justice Center, Kitsap County Jail, and Portland Jail—thank you for feeding me and keeping me safe. Likewise, to the staff of the James Oldham Treatment Center and American Behavioral Health Systems Specialty Services II—thank you for doing the same while giving me insightful clean time that eventually accrued to a determining point at which I never looked back (except to write this book).

To my Kitsap County Public Defender, who saw my potential behind the drug-fueled bravado. I'm grateful that you steered me away from prison and toward drug court.

To my Kitsap County Drug Court team—you all gave this estranged and wayward soul a surrogate family, modeling for me the meaning of emotional stability and availability, which I internalized to reparent myself. Without you all, the last section of this book would not exist.

To my South Kitsap County recovery community—every person in the 12-Step meetings in Port Orchard, Bremerton, and Key Peninsula (technically Pierce County but close enough), the Hewitt Oxford House, God's Broken Home University, the Vineyard Homes of Compassion, the Clevenger Eagles Wings, the KCDCAA Better Perspective House, Joe Mama's House, and the Westside Clean and Sober Softball Association comprise the village that raised my inner child to become a man with the wherewithal to write this book.

To Melody Beattie, Tara Brach, Brené Brown, Carl Jung, Gabor Maté, David Graeber, David Wengrow, Daniel Z. Lieberman, Michael E. Long, Robert Sternberg, my Human Services professors at Olympic College, and the authors of the Adult Children of Alcoholics & Dysfunctional Families, Codependents Anonymous, and NA texts, who gave me the power to recognize, allow, investigate, and nurture the forces inside me. Your knowledge gave this book the profundity that lived experience cannot provide on its own.

To the original Homey Corps team, who not only believed in my crazy idea, but also allowed me to experience for the first time what it means to be credible. Thank you for letting me write this book as part of the organization's strategic vision.

To the Washington State Department of Commerce Reentry Grant team, for awarding Homey Corps a grant to launch full-time operations—you all put my social service agency on the map, giving me the confidence to write this book with a neat and inspirational ending.

To my publisher, for deciding to join the Silverdale Rotary Club the very day I presented at a monthly meeting as my token of appreciation for their donation to Homey Corps. Wrapping up my presentation, I talked about wanting to write my memoir to advocate for formerly incarcerated homeless people with substance use and co-occurring disorders, and to use as a marketing vehicle to attract charitable partnerships with national retailers. When my publisher approached me after the meeting and said, "I'm interested in your book," I knew it was a divine appointment.

To Pete—without your consistent encouragement (badgering?) to write my story, I'm not sure I would have undertaken this project.

To my birth family, who greeted their prodigal son and brother with open arms—thank you for keeping me in that embrace since my return (especially my father and mother, who never let go) and giving me the emotional permission to write this book.

Finally, to the em dash—my favorite punctuation mark, which I will wield with flourish for as long as I write.

Foreword

by the Publisher

At Kitsap Publishing, we believe in amplifying voices that matter—especially those rooted in local truth and transformation. For years, we've been privileged to publish stories that reflect the complex realities of our region: its struggles, resilience, and humanity.

Professional Drug Addict is one of those stories. This gripping memoir is not only a raw account of addiction, homelessness, and crime—it's a deeply human journey of recovery, redemption, and purpose. Arnel Castro Leyva offers an unflinching look into a world many pretend not to see, and in doing so, he gives voice to the silenced and hope to the forgotten.

As a publisher deeply involved in Kitsap County's civic and cultural life, we are proud to bring this book to print. It speaks directly to issues we care about—restorative justice, substance abuse recovery, housing instability, and the power of second chances.

This is not just a memoir. It's a call to see differently, act more boldly, and believe in what's possible when people are given the support they need to rise.

We are honored to stand behind *Professional Drug Addict*, and we hope it reaches everyone who needs to hear its message.

Ingemar Anderson
Publisher, Kitsap Publishing

Introduction

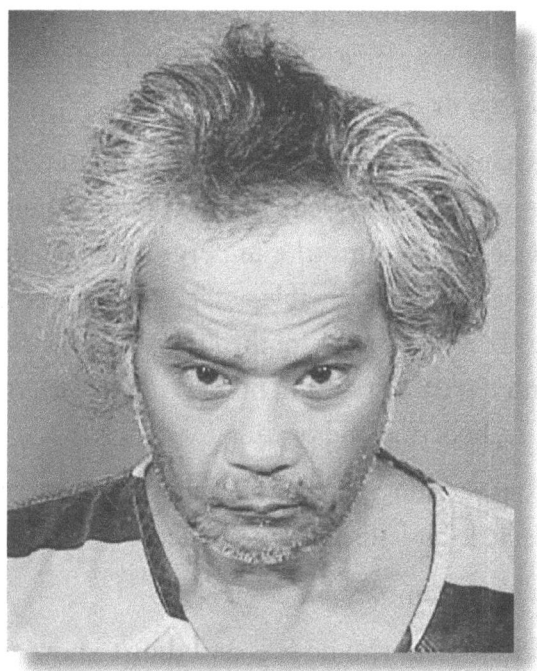

November 2020

That's my last booking photo.

It was taken two months before I entered Kitsap County Drug Court—a prison-diversion program that allows people charged with drug-related felonies to serve their time in the community under strict judicial supervision, while receiving intensive addiction treatment.

That booking photo is the culmination of a two-year run on the streets as a homeless criminal drug addict—the government-mandated and professional term is "person with substance use disorder," but that's such a mouthful—I choose to use the less polite expression as my way of reclaiming the power of a derogatory term.

Before my two-year run and that mugshot, I'd built a 25-year career in the technology industry, working for Microsoft, T-Mobile, Adobe, Yahoo, and a handful of startups, agencies, and consultancies in Seattle, Silicon Valley, Los Angeles, San Diego, Portland, and Scotland, living in the higher median-income parts of town, while getting high in the parking garage of my office building to self-medicate my social anxiety, believing that my drug use fueled my success.

Then my unmanageable double life became intolerable—my house was foreclosed, my car repossessed, and my family, friends, and associates estranged. I descended into the underground full-time, arriving with nothing except my most valuable asset—the look of the establishment that initially allowed me to roam through retail stores and urban neighborhoods unfettered. I stayed in hotels and motels, then bus stops and encampments, boosting and trading for drugs.

Looking at that version of me now, I'm no longer overcome with shame. There's still a little bit—it's not my best look.

What I feel now is compassion.

That guy had no idea who he was and didn't know any better. He was never taught how to regulate his emotions—he either lost his temper or took drugs; there wasn't much emotional nuance in between.

He also had no ethics or integrity. He had morals—he wouldn't kill people or steal money out of their pocket. But he would take it out of their bank account or charge up a storm on their credit cards. He wasn't hurting anyone, just scamming the system. Right?

To that guy, the ends always justified the means—he did whatever it took to get what he thought he wanted, regardless of the repercussions, consequences, and injury to others.

That guy also didn't know that he was already on the path to enlightenment, and that this path would involve an ancient ritualistic process that would prepare him to become a community leader.

I'll explain what I mean with a short history lesson.

The commonly held belief of how democratic representative governments were founded in the United States is that the colonists came here, bringing with them the Greek ideals of democracy and the Roman template for republics, and implemented these principles on this supposedly uncivilized soil.

However, a new school of archaeology and anthropology, espoused in the book *The Dawn of Everything*, has revisited this evidence and arrived at a very different conclusion. This new school posits that representative governments already existed amongst the civilizations of ancient America. These concepts, radical in their exaltation of individual rights that in parallel supported the community, were then brought back to Europe, along with coffee, and were discussed in these newfangled places called cafes, which birthed the Age of Enlightenment, from which the Declaration of Independence and the Constitution were born.

One of these ancient civilizations was the Tlaxcala in Central America, adjacent to the Mayans and Aztecs. How they elected their community leaders differed significantly from our system—they didn't hold elections to vote for the candidate they thought was the most charismatic figure, as we do.

Instead, if someone in the community dared to show the ambition and arrogance to become a community leader, the first thing the Tlaxcala did was subject them to rituals of public humiliation. The Tlaxcala believed that leaders must serve their people and be subservient. So, let's wring every last bit of self-centeredness out of them first.

After that, the Tlaxcala elders would isolate the self-centered would-be leaders in the woods and subject them to rituals of bloodletting, fasting, and sleep deprivation. If the initiates were still standing, they were further subjected to a regimen of strict moral training.

If our promising leaders made it through all that successfully, they were taken back to the community and presented as having been prepared and ready to serve as community leaders.

Now, let's apply this ancient ritualistic process to my life as a homeless criminal drug addict...

Public Humiliation: Every day—homeless criminal drug addicts are the Untouchables of the American caste system, systematically excluded from resources and opportunities, and forced to live off the waste of a wasteful society.

Isolation: Homeless criminal drug addicts are isolated in plain sight—no one looks us in the eye; the mainstream pretend we don't exist—otherwise, they'd have to question their own existence.

Bloodletting: Every time I used a needle to shoot up.

Fasting: Who needs food? Drugs fueled me.

Sleep Deprivation: Same thing—up for days on end, fueled by drugs.

Driven by methamphetamine, I forced my body to stay awake days on end, catching sleep intermittently while standing still or sleepwalking, because of two ongoing goals: 1) Avoiding downtime hustling after currency to buy or trade for my drug of choice; 2) Protecting the currency I had already acquired.

Currency is most effective as cold, hard cash. But for boosters (those who make their living from shoplifting, a demographic that also includes porch pirates and car prowlers—those who steal online shopping packages left on porches and in mailboxes, as well as break into cars in parking lots and residences), currency mainly takes the form of consumer goods that their drug dealers, family members, friends, and fellow bus riders find desirable—the newest sneakers, leisure wear, personal electronics, power tools, even steaks and seafood.

My fellow boosters and I would continually show off our revolving stock of currency to our target market by employing two methods simultaneously: 1) Advertising stock by wearing it, price tags dangling while walking down bus aisles but hidden to look the part when walking through any retail door and neighborhood; 2) Staying mobile, which meant carrying no more than two backpacks that could be stashed away from the envious gazes of homeless scavengers.

The most effective boosters avoid carrying cumbersome, unsightly camping gear, which results in rotating overnight stays between a welcoming group of encampments and cheap motels on Highway 99 when I've hit a 'lick'—property crimes committed in the surrounding neighborhoods, resulting in a stash of cash beyond what I needed to get that night's fix.

Most of the time, I found it much more efficient and economical to abstain from sleep and instead obtain a continuous stream of drugs to stay up for days.

Until I would invariably 'fall out'—the point beyond fatigue, where taking even more drugs could not keep me conscious. I would fall into a deep sleep from which no rousing could wake me before my body could recharge.

At this point, the homeless vultures and hyenas descended upon my stash of goods. When I finally came to, all the currency that I had hustled for and protected 24/7 was gone. What had been a relative trickle of obtaining just enough goods to barter for drugs and look good doing it became a veritable crime spree.

I would usually get caught by a store's loss prevention team when I reached the level of post-fallout desperation. My newfound energy and anger at the world made me act conspicuously, stealing too many items at once. I would end up catching a case, wherein store detectives tracked the number of thefts I had previously committed in a specific store until the combined value reached the city ordinance's felony level.

If I got caught with a backpack selected from the store stuffed with an armload of wares, I might be charged with a misdemeanor. I might supplement my boosting with a bit of mail-boxing and porch-pirating around a neighborhood, happen upon an unlocked car with the spare key in the glove compartment, and take off. I'd get caught, charged with another felony, and taken to jail. During the COVID-era lockdown, the police would release me from custody because the jails were usually over capacity.

I consistently missed court dates because the court summons would have been sent to my last known address, which I had quit years ago.

And on and on...

My final act of desperation was an unsanctioned shopping spree at Target in Renton, WA. Boosters use a trick to evade loss prevention teams—we arrive right when the store opens because the loss prevention staff start their shift one hour later. I hardly took anything worthwhile that day compared to my more brazen shopping trips in the past—a winter coat for me and a tent that someone in one of the encampments on Highway 99 would find valuable enough to trade for a bit of meth.

However, the area where this Target was located—a well-to-do mixed-use complex called Renton Landing—was difficult to escape because seemingly everyone was part of the neighborhood watch club. Everywhere I went to hide, some do-gooder apartment dweller pulled up and parked...in front of me. I trekked to one of the bus stops and prayed for a bus to arrive just in time. Instead, a police car pulled up.

"You've got about 10 warrants for your arrest, Mr. Leyva," the policeman drawled as he put handcuffs on me.

He drove me to the SCORE jail, where I donned the jail stripes in my final booking photo, and was extradited to Kitsap County.

Strict Moral Training: An effective way to solidify recovery from drug addiction, the way to make it stick, is by being subjected to a strict moral program. And by "subjected," I mean surrendering to it. My strict moral program was Kitsap County Drug Court.

During my first year, I found my calling and the startup idea I had been chasing my entire career—helping other homeless drug addicts find a new life in a sustainable and scalable solution underwritten by the business community. But the formula for the unique value proposition that I was seeking remained just beyond my grasp until I got a sponsor who guided me through the 12 Steps. We discussed my business idea and honed it into a concept called Loss Prevention as a Social Good.

Less than 30% of addicts and alcoholics get into recovery; of that fortunate few, less than 30% remain in recovery. Compare those statistics to the Drug Court graduation rate, which is around 90%. That is unparalleled in the world of criminal justice rehabilitation programs. However, the data analysis I'd like to see is the rate of Drug Court graduates who remain in recovery. Based on anecdotal evidence, that rate falls back down below 30%. The difference between the fortunate minority and the majority that fall by the wayside is a continuation of a strict moral program.

I created my own strict moral program that houses, stabilizes, and educates justice-involved people with substance use and co-occurring disorders, with the goal of hiring our clients who make it successfully through our program and receive a bachelor's degree. This goal underscores the overriding principle of all 12-Step fellowships—we can only keep what we have by giving it away.

I went from flying high in the corporate world to getting high every day and committing crimes to sustain that high. I can't go back to either. I've seen too much.

Now, the Untouchables of the American caste system are the people with whom I choose to work and surround myself.

This book is about how I realized that at my lowest point, I was already on the path to enlightenment, where I found my people and the calling that had eluded me throughout my previous career.

The stories and concepts on the following pages recount my descent into and eventual rise from the life of a homeless criminal drug addict. I will do my best to recount what happened, when, and why. I can't guarantee that everything will be presented precisely as it happened. But this is how it all happened.

November 2024

The carport in the photo above connects the little house and the big house that make up Joe Mama's House, the recovery residence where Homey Corps—the social service agency that I launched in July 2024—places our clients and provides them with rental assistance. Like the tenants, the owner is also formerly incarcerated and in recovery—he opened the house as a tribute to his older brother, whose street name was Joemama and died of an opioid overdose. I used to live here—moved out one year before finishing the manuscript for this book. The sustainable recovery lifestyle I developed during my three years living in a series of recovery residences informed this book and the development of Homey Corps' program lifecycle, which is designed to stabilize our clients and provide them with tangible hope for a living-wage recovery.

PART I

Descent

Chapter 1

Girlfriend Experience

GFE (Girlfriend Experience): A commercial sex service, which usually entails transactional sex between client and escort, and may include physical acts associated with emotional intimacy, such as kissing or unprotected sex.

I had a thing for escorts.

The transactional promise of sex with no strings when I was high and alone in my house, which is how I preferred to get high, and the need to be with someone just long enough to quench my thirst for human interaction (but no longer than the moment that thirst was quenched) always sounded like the perfect proposition at the time.

I like to say that Diana was my first GFE. It's my way of positioning whatever it was that she and I had somewhere between a traditional girlfriend and the standard transaction between client and escort. There is no exclusivity with escorts, even if they seem to prefer spending time with you over anyone else. Having multiple men around generates a diversified revenue stream, which is how successful escorts make a living.

A woman I would meet about a year after I met Diana stated that she could never understand how prostitutes could take money for sex. This woman and I were stuck in the apartment of a mutual friend-crony-supplier who was out making his rounds, delivering his highly sought-after mind-altering and mood-enhancing products to his clientele from Everett to Kirkland to Renton. We expected him back in Wallingford, a civilized community near the University of Washington, in the wee hours of the morning. Until his return, this woman and I took as much of the meth he had left us as we felt comfortable taking, and we felt comfortable. This woman was attractive, although not enough to overcome her holier-than-thou attitude.

"Let's say you meet a guy and you like him. How much money does he usually have to spend—taking you out for dinner, drinks, clubbing, maybe he wants to show how cultured he is and even takes you to a play, oh, and drugs—how much does he have to spend before you let him fuck you? $400? $500?" I paused for effect. "So, that's the price you'd ask your client upfront."

Her gaze turned cold.

I'd made my point. We didn't talk much after that.

Diana, on the other hand, was so good at her profession that she didn't need to provide sex to get paid per transaction. She had a guy living in the Boston suburbs paying her rent on the other side of the country for a sublet apartment in Bainbridge Island.

In this bedroom community, highly paid workers take the 35-minute ferry ride across Puget Sound to work in Seattle and surrounding suburbs, then sail back across to eat with their families and sleep. Legend has it that one of the Amazon cofounders lived there on the down low—he drove around in an old truck. Supposedly, a few of the Tupper family members, flush for the rest of their lives because of their association with Tupperware, lived down the gravel road from the glamping-quality log cabin I stayed in during my first year there. Bainbridge Island is so posh, it isn't just a leafy suburb—it is a forest community that will remain that way as long as the Bainbridge Island Trust stops property development of the large parcels of land they own and are sworn to preserve.

That's where I found Diana, subletting an apartment that seemed a nice enough place, but only in comparison to the quality of the entire island could it be classified as the ghetto.

The first night I arrived on her doorstep, I was at the casino with Jake (his older brother had sublet the apartment to Diana). I was sitting at a slot machine, bored and antsy, so I asked Jake if he knew where we could get cocaine. I had snorted a line of crushed Adderall before going to the casino, but it was wearing off.

I was taking a chance asking Jake that question.

I had needed help moving furniture into my cabin located steps from Battle Point Park and nestled next to Fairy Dell Trail—the asymmetry of these names was indicative of my double life—and answered Jake's Craigslist ad for moving services. Jake lived in a big house in the town of Suquamish. He and his wife lived off her Amazon stock—she had started with the company when it was relatively young and stuck it out long enough to live a life of relative luxury. Jake liked to keep physically busy. I could tell he was unorthodox.

"Here, take this." Jake pulled a little baggie from his pocket and handed it to me.

"What is it?"

"Try it."

"Should I go to the car and make a line?"

"Just eat it," Jake urged.

I thought it might be meth. I'd never done it before. I was a coke man. And before that, ecstasy. I looked down my nose at speed and its ilk.

The template for my lifestyle as a professional drug addict started when I was freshly graduated from the University of Washington and helped launch an underground music magazine, Hype, with a few friends from high school. Grunge was just becoming a movement, and some of us were English majors who wanted to hang out, get drunk, smoke weed, see our writing published, and get into music shows for free. One time, Nirvana played a show at Beehive Records, when record stores were the hub of the subculture. The band had just released *Nevermind*. I wrote a review about the show—they were okay. Little did I know at the time.

My first startup enterprise, fueled by substance use and the prevailing subculture, lasted about three years before we started to disintegrate out of disinterest.

I landed a job with Aldus, the originator of desktop publishing, and used the company's resources to design and create master prints of our monthly publication. Before the internet, desktop publishing seemed like a miracle—anyone with access to a computer and laser printer could lay out a magazine in just a few hours.

Aldus started paying me pretty well when Adobe acquired it. I turned this corporate transition into a job in Edinburgh, Scotland, with the localization agency contracted to translate and produce European versions of Adobe software. Ever since my post-collegiate solo European excursion, trekking through Britain and Western Europe on Eurail, when I tried in vain to find a job as an au pair with an aristocracy-adjacent family in Paris, I knew I wanted to live in a European city to add an adventurous sojourn to my professional resume.

I would live in Edinburgh for two years. I consider the city my second home. I toiled through a year learning how to drink whiskey to survive the cold and work long hours because I had no friends—didn't really enjoy drinking, and had nothing else to do. Then I met a rag-tag faction of nascent professionals with members from up and down the UK who worked during the week and spent long weekends clubbing and drugging. They introduced me to ecstasy. It changed my life. Its main ingredient, MDMA, was leveraged by marriage counselors during couples' sessions to allow feuding partners to overcome their erstwhile unbreakable tension.

Ecstasy allowed me to get over my insecurities and connect with people in a foreign land, let go of the self-consciousness that I had fostered throughout my childhood as an immigrant to the U.S., which had become more pronounced as a dark American in Edinburgh, and join the throbbing mass of fit, young, good-looking, cosmopolitan club-goers in the mid-1990's.

It was during this era of my addiction when I was ordained into the Order of the Professional Drug Addicts.

The best ecstasy, in my summation, is a concoction of MDMA, cocaine, and a little bit of heroin. This cocktail is best paired with lines of cocaine on the side. I'm sure most ecstasy concoctions include a little bit of speed, but I never admitted that to myself. Speed was too low-class for me and my mates.

That is, until I met Diana.

Eating meth, rather than smoking or shooting it, takes about 30 minutes to digest before it hits. When it hit the first time, my lethargy and boredom were completely cured. I had been diagnosed with adult ADD a few years back, which is why I had an Adderall prescription that eventually didn't do enough for me, finally resorting to crushing and snorting it. Stimulants perk me up a little, but mainly they calm my mind, give me focus, and make everything seem alright. That's exactly how I felt when the meth took effect, but an order of magnitude more alright.

Where had this elixir been all my life?

"Got any more?"

"All out."

"Where can we get more?"

Jake paused and then motioned for me to follow him. We hopped into his truck and drove to the only block on Bainbridge Island that could be considered a ghetto.

Diana answered the door to the apartment that Jake's brother had vacated for six months because he was on a job out of town. She was staying there because she wanted to spend time with her stepmother, who was in the final stages of cancer and lived with her family in Port Angeles, a town situated on the Strait of Juan de Fuca. Since Diana lived in Portland and would rather not have to give up doing drugs at her leisure while staying with her family, subletting a vacated apartment and being everyone's plug was the type of serendipity that seemed to befall her regularly.

On the way to Diana's apartment, Jake told me she made her money as an escort. Check.

Diana was wearing shorts when she answered the door—I'm a leg man, so I first noticed her shapely legs, proportionately long for her body, with a fetching ratio of softness and muscularity. Check.

She came from Swedish heritage, and when I say Swedish, I mean she looked like the Swedes I encountered while touring Europe—the Olympic and Kitsap Peninsulas were settled by Norwegians and Swedes; the cold climate, evergreen trees, and numerous canals (fjords by another name) made the settlers feel at home; and the Puget Sound acted as a natural barrier to the melting pot of the mainland mixing with the Nordic stock. Check.

When we settled into the living room, Diana pulled out a bong with a mixture of ice and water in the chamber, and a big shard of meth in the bowl. Check.

I asked about the ice water. Diana said that its purpose is to cool down the meth smoke. I took a long drag off the bong—it was refreshing, and the effect seemed instantaneous compared to eating the little shard that Jake gave me earlier.

Where has this stuff, and Diana, been all my life?

I had brought only $20 to the casino. I wasn't much of a gambler back then—never won anything, so I had no idea of the insidious effects of winning. My mother was a big gambler, but I always thought that gene had skipped over me. I had lost my money instantly on the slot machines and stopped playing. I didn't have any cash when we got to Diana's place, so I traded her a handful of Adderall pills for a nice-sized shard. If you know an Adderall buyer, selling them can be more lucrative than cocaine, and much more than meth—this exchange was designed to buy her loyalty.

I texted Diana while lying in bed, as calm as a summer lake in the early morning, yet buzzing like a madman.

ME: "I have never been so high in my life."

DIANA: lol

ME: "Wanna hang out tomorrow?"

DIANA: "Just hit me up."

This was the first time I had met an escort off duty. I was excited to see if I could develop a friendship that wouldn't dead-end in the friend zone.

And I wanted more of her drugs.

* * *

I would visit Diana at the apartment every day during the first week we met.

I discovered that she had trained herself to be an astute marketer—she was a natural photographer, taking intriguing selfies that showed the right amount of face to personalize photos, but insufficient to completely identify herself, while showing enough skin to titillate her audience without being crass; she stayed off the free escort sites and marketed herself exclusively on the paid sites, as she knew that a higher percentage of established men could be found on there; she had become an expert market sizer, identifying in which cities she should post her ads to get the best conversion rate based on the population (demand) and number of ads already posted in that market (supply).

Diana had a boyfriend who had gotten into trouble and was sent to prison a couple of months before we met. He would be gone for a few years, and she wasn't sure what would happen between them. So, she had a criminal sort-of boyfriend locked up and an East Coast businessman sugar daddy 3000 miles away.

"With me, you now have an everyday combination of those two motherfuckers."

She liked that.

After the average amount of time had passed that it usually takes mainstream people who actually like each other to spend enough time together and to broach the subject of sex, Diana broached in her own way.

"I'm used to getting money."

"I know." I wanted to take care of Diana the way her East Coast sugar daddy did, but I also didn't want to feel taken, and I didn't have the same resources. "Maybe we can make an ongoing deal. I'll take care of some of your expenses, give you some things, and we can keep a tally until it reaches, say, $300?"

"A pussy kitty!"

I laughed and coughed as I finished taking a hit from the bong. I reached into my coat pocket, retrieved my freshly filled prescription bottle of Adderall, and poured out 20 pills into my hand.

"Here. Those go for at least $20 each on the streets. Since you have to do the selling, let's apply a pussy-kitty premium by discounting their value by three-quarters, so that's a $100 value into the pussy kitty."

"Deal." Diana shook my hand.

The next day, Diana told me she had to leave town for two days. She confided that, when she's away, she doesn't answer texts: Out of sight, out of mind. I didn't understand—I write paragraphs if I'm interested in a woman, regardless of where she might be. I wanted to seal our commitment with a kiss. But we never kissed. Too intimate.

"Do you have PayPal?" I asked.

"Yeah. Why?"

"I wanna give you pussy-kitty gas money for your trip" I sent her $100. Then I left.

Diana reached out a couple of days later. I'd been trying to figure out how to make up that last $100 in value, so that we could set up a date. I had it all planned out—we'd get a suite at the casino; she'd bring a bag full of meth and in return for smoking as much I wanted, I'd give her

$100 to gamble with, which should be enough for both of us because she was a good gambler, and I didn't get much out of it.

"How did your ad perform?" I had helped her write the copy for her latest escort ad on a paid escort site and instructed her to post it in the Bainbridge Island section, as there were no ads targeted to that area.

"I got a date offa there. The guy was really nice. But he said I shouldn't advertise in Bainbridge anymore because the cops here don't like that."

"Did he pay well?" I asked. Diana nodded her head. "Well, then. Since I helped you get that business, that's at least $100 of value, if you apply the pussy-kitty premium. That makes $300 in the pussy kitty." I harbored resentment that I needed her to remedy.

"Okay." Diana pursed her lips and squinted her eyes, then revealed a tiny smile.

During our date, Diana gave me the best hand job I have ever experienced in my entire life. That statement still holds today. While I was on top of her in bed, she took hold of me before I could even try to enter her, and I stopped in mid-action because the way she held me was as good as being inside another woman. She told me later that her modus operandi is to either wait to have sex all the way or continue providing hand jobs if she's not into the guy. To that end, she became one of the world's foremost experts at hand jobs.

I have never experienced anything like an orgasm while high on meth. Even after years in recovery, I believe that this level of sexual intensity exclusive to meth orgasms is a foundational factor to my becoming a born-again virgin (commitment before consummation). I'm afraid that casual natural sex can never compete, or even approach, the preternatural force of meth sex.

It would be five years later, during my first college course in the substance use disorder professional certificate program at Olympic College, that I would understand the clinical reason behind meth sex. The graph below shows the nanomoles per liter (nM) of dopamine produced by different activities…

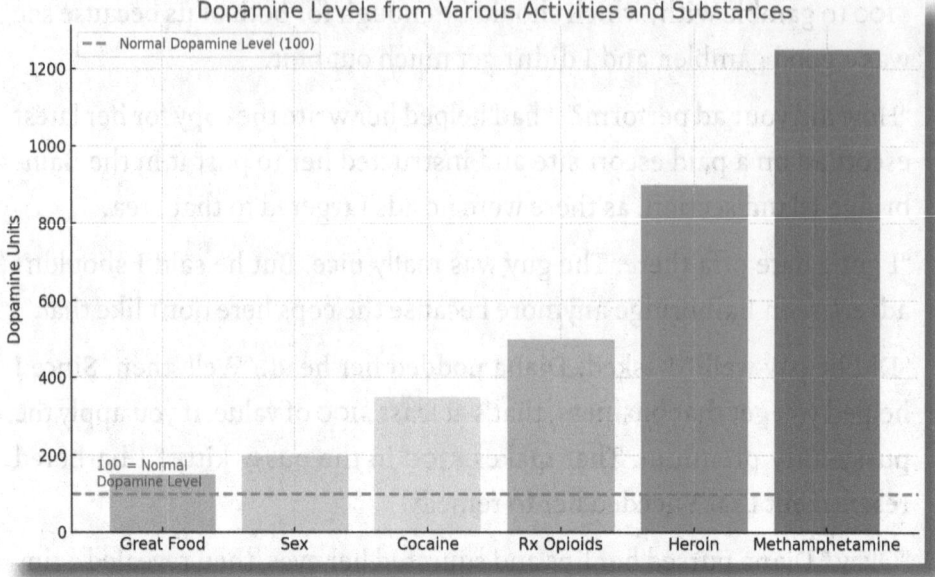

Data reference from https://www.chronicleonline.com.

Dopamine is called the "feel-good" neurotransmitter. It is the source of the beneficent adjective "dope." The feel-good aspect is fundamental to our existence—we all need a certain amount of dopamine (the "100 = normal dopamine level" in the graphic above) just to have the gumption to get out of bed and not kill ourselves. In fact, people with clinical depression have been shown to have lower levels of baseline dopamine than the general population.

When I learned that meth produces 1300 nM of dopamine—6.5 times that of sex; 3.5 times that of cocaine; 1.5 times that of heroin; and unlike those drugs, there exist meth recipes that can keep your cock hard—I thought to myself, "Why isn't everyone hooked on it?" And I understood the insidious allure of meth's feel-good power—it is the most potent dopamine generator ever created by humankind.

That's why I, as someone with off-kilter brain chemistry that causes attention deficit disorder, love it.

This graph also substantiates the existence of food and sex addicts—any drug or activity that yields dopamine beyond normal production levels has the potential to become a disorder. This phenomenon occurs because our brains aren't wired to handle supernormally prolonged dopamine exposure. Our bodies naturally seek equilibrium, and the brain does this against an overabundance of neurotransmitters by shutting down receptors exclusive to each neurotransmitter—an addict's brain becomes less receptive to dopamine because there's usually too much of it for the brain to handle.

Here's the insidious part—because of the decreased receptivity, the baseline (or normal) dopamine level of an addict is lowered, so when they're not high on food-sex-coke-meth, they have the dopamine level of someone clinically depressed. This is why addicts are so driven to get more—they need their drug or activity of choice just to get back to everyone's normal level.

After meth sex, regular sex for me will remain below normal people's baseline. I'm going to need love to accompany sex to give it a chance of being any good. That means I'll need to learn what love actually, truly is.

I wouldn't learn that with Diana.

But we liked each other in a way that escorts and clients aren't supposed to do. When Diana's East Coast sugar daddy came for his one and only visit while we were together, he got a room for them at the casino. I was so jealous that I was surprised and disappointed with myself. I wasn't supposed to feel like this about an escort—we were hanging out; I knew the rules. What I couldn't stand more than anything else was that her sugar had the resources to put her up in an apartment, and I did not. The day after her rendezvous to pay her rent, Diana told me that she pretended to be on her period and could only give him a hand job—I appreciated the gesture regardless of how hard I tried to see it as insufficient.

Diana had a five-year-old son. His father was one of the biggest meth dealers in the Portland area. She had quit smoking meth and cigarettes during her pregnancy to ensure that her son would be born healthy. Still, Child Protective Services had seized him when she got into trouble; she spent a year after that meeting the agency's requirements, including staying clean off drugs, attending parenting classes, and keeping a clean record—she earned her son back. After the first couple of weeks of our affair, Diana began allowing her son to be present when I visited; we'd often go grocery shopping or do laundry together. Diana and her son gave me a taste of the domesticity I had been craving, but didn't know I needed.

However, my inferiority complex with Mr. East Coast businessman would be our demise.

He flew her to the East Coast to visit him, covering the cost of a week in a hotel in Boston. When Diana returned, she was sporting a designer handbag. She must have seen the look on my face when I noticed it because she started recounting her week by telling me how every time he tried to have sex with her, she told him that she was on her period. I bet that just drove him crazier and crazier for her.

A week after her Boston escapade, Diana abruptly informed me that she was moving back to Portland...in two days. Her stepmother had died in hospice, Jake's brother was returning to live in the apartment, and a friend of hers had an extra room in which he would let her stay until she found a place.

Everything always fell into place for Diana.

I visited Diana in Portland two weeks later. She had arranged for her cousin to babysit her kid. We stayed in a hotel, she brought a quarter ounce of meth, and we went to a sex shop where I bought a toy of her choosing. The guy who owned the house where she and her kid stayed kept calling and texting her, asking where she was, what she was doing, when she'd be back, and if she didn't return when promised, he'd put her stuff on the sidewalk. Obviously, he had a crush on her, but he was stuck in her not merely friend zone, but an even worse place: her useful friend zone—there is no way out of there.

The sex toy was meant for couples—it had two pads, one for each person's genitalia, and a remote control that supplied a low-level, continuous electric shock. Diana liked it...a lot—she kept using it while I lay naked in bed next to her. I didn't like it…at all. So, I ripped the pad off myself and watched her obsessively press the button and shiver. I felt like the odd man out in a threesome. When she fell asleep, she let me have my way with her bareback.

I didn't feel like a third wheel anymore. I was her respite from an oppressive home environment, her savior.

Did I say that things always fell into place for Diana? A week later, she informed me that she'd be moving into a two-bedroom apartment in a leafy suburb of Portland—her sugar was paying for the whole thing. She invited me to visit a few weeks after she had packed, moved in, and settled.

I took the train from Seattle to Portland. I like taking trains—they invoke a romanticism that will never wane. Diana's new apartment was a nice spot in a nice area, which made me uncomfortable. She had a lot of nice things to furnish the place—she had kept everything in storage, knowing that this occasion would happen sometime. She made it happen.

We watched television the night I arrived. Diana's kid sat next to me on the sofa—he put one arm on my shoulder and peered at whatever I was reading. It was a sweet gesture. Diana didn't want to have sex while her kid was around. I tried when we were alone in her bathroom, but she demurred. We were supposed to stay in a hotel the next night to get high and have sex all night, but I left the next day. I didn't want to be there. She didn't need me to save her anymore.

I told Diana I had to leave, gaslighting her by saying I'd told her I was coming to Portland for just one night. She dropped me off at Union Station. I couldn't tell her that I didn't want to see her anymore. I'd wait for her to text me and then tell her.

Diana is the picture of the escort in control—she trafficked herself and made a suburban living out of it.

But there was a woman at the train station who epitomized the other side of the human-trafficking spectrum, waiting for someone to protect her. I didn't think that someone would be me when I asked her for a lighter—I had been fumbling through my pockets and couldn't find one. I approached her with my unlit cigarette in hand, as she was sitting in the outdoor waiting area away from the station entrance. At first glance, I couldn't identify her gender—she was so skinny that I couldn't make out hips and breasts, but she also didn't have the shoulders to identify as a man instantly. Her face could have been that of a prepubescent boy or a bulimic woman. Her hair was cropped short. When she handed me her lighter, she gave me a tired smile, longing for genuine attention from someone kind. After so many things unsaid in my goodbye to Diana, I didn't have any attention to give anyone. So, I thanked her and smoked my cigarette on the other side of the waiting area.

I went into the station and found the line for the Seattle train. As I was waiting, I saw the same woman exit the restroom. She saw me standing in line.

"Is this the train to Seattle?" she asked.

"Yeah. Thanks again for the light," I said.

She got in line behind me, and we got to talking. It didn't take long for her to start telling me her sad and sordid story—she was on her way to Seattle to stay at a women's shelter where a friend from high school was a resident aide. This godsend had all come together so quickly, she felt blessed after the horror of having been kidnapped by some guys from whom she used to buy meth in Eugene, about an hour and a half drive from Portland—they had kept her captive in a motel room and continuously drugged up; they hardly fed her; she didn't remember much except a hazy line of guys having sex with her; she was so weak and constantly drugged that she couldn't do anything to stop it; she finally managed to escape one day when her captors had become too comfortable and left her alone; she stumbled out of the motel room in a daze. Her story faded out after that.

She concluded that her captors might still be looking for her—they wanted to make sure she didn't say anything to the authorities.

A part of me thought she was setting me up for a scam. But the more expansive part of me believed her. Her voice and how she looked away with a hint of embarrassment after telling her story were authentic. How she could know that I, out of all the people waiting in that train station, would perhaps be the only person who could grasp her plight was beyond me.

"You're with me now. You're going to sit with me on the train. We're going to stay in the public eye the whole time. I don't give a shit how big and dangerous these guys might be. They can't pull any shit in public."

We rode together the entire journey. I told her about my weekend cut short with Diana. She told me about how people in Eugene would just come up to her on the streets and ask if she had a bubble (meth pipe) they could use, and how her uncle used to cook meth in the backyard. She'd been in The Life for so long that some bitter and judgmental people in polite society might think she had invited whatever had befallen her by living her degenerate life.

"Maybe this was my fault," she lamented.

"No. It's not. And I'm going to make sure you arrive safely."

I only let her out of my sight the three times that I went to the restroom to crush up and snort a line of meth. I rushed back each time, wondering whether I'd find one of her kidnappers sitting next to her, whispering in her ear, while she sat frozen with a look of quiet horror on her face. But she was safe every time I stumbled across the train aisle.

As the train pulled into King Street Station, she turned to me.

"I want to keep in touch, but I don't have a phone. Maybe you could give your number to one of the girls from the house?"

I wanted to know how she was doing—her progress would reflect my good deed. There's a derogatory but very fitting term for a man with the urge to save damsels of the night in distress: Captain Save-a-Ho. That was me.

We walked through the crowd until she spotted her old friend and the crew from the women's shelter. Her old friend looked at me sternly.

"Who are you?" Her old friend sized me up.

I explained that her friend had asked for my help at the train station, and I had protected her during the trip. I reached into my coat pocket to retrieve my phone. I pulled up my LinkedIn profile to prove my legitimacy—the same profile that I had nurtured and cultivated to develop my online presence ever since I had become one of the first 100,000 members back in 2003; the profile that displayed the breadth and depth of my noteworthy business background; the very same profile that I would send to the prostitutes whom I would woo over multiple texts to close the deal.

"I just want to know she's alright."

Her friend's face softened. "We got her now."

Chapter 2

The Life

Kaylee was a captivating gatekeeper at the entry to the underground.

She could have been the next-door neighbor's daughter in the predominantly white suburban neighborhood where I grew up. She might have graduated from the University of Washington, where she would have served as an officer in her sorority. Because of her traditional beauty and razor-sharp intelligence, it would surprise no one who had ever looked at her and listened to her polite version if she had leveraged her sorority network to land an entry-level job at Microsoft. It would seem only natural that the vice president of her business unit had already begun including her as part of his away team at business meetings to distract the men on the other side of the table during negotiations with different business units within Microsoft, or perhaps at pitch sessions to would-be clients, thus giving the VP an advantage before talks even began.

Corporate men of means instinctively surrounded themselves with Kaylee's level of youth and beauty to rejuvenate themselves and put their opponents (or would-be partners) on the defensive.

I found Kaylee on Backpage. Before the moral minority shut down this illustrious online publication by accusing its publishers with aiding and abetting human trafficking, Backpage was the place to find your girlfriend experience (GFE) in the safety of your own home. The women were known as "escorts," different from prostitutes because they didn't walk the streets and preferred regulars rather than one-night transactions (at least, that's how escorts claimed to differentiate themselves). Escort sites allowed Kaylee—and other women with her level of digital savvy gleaned from a lifetime of experience—to be their own marketers and agents. It gave them the autonomy to traffic themselves from the relative safety of their motel room or car.

As Facebook was turning scrolling into the world's favorite pastime and Tinder turned swiping into foreplay, brazen escort sites allowed hobbyists (that's what johns, or clients, call themselves—whereas Kaylee and her ilk called their transactions "dates") to scroll through a bevy of available women in the surrounding area. I'm not sure of the exact percentage of listings that were put up by pimps, but from what I could gather from my marketing expertise, every listing I scrolled through, and which attracted me, seemed like the work of the subject. As I was a product marketing executive with a global technology company when I found Kaylee, I knew something about authenticity in marketing.

There was also something very familiar about the type of women who became call girls. One of the characteristics that these women often used to describe themselves on escort sites and Craigslist Casual Encounters (back in its prime before the same moral minority banded together for the first time to take down a highly efficient and decentralized marketplace to sell oneself) was "people-pleaser." When guys read that, it conjures the image of a young, vulnerable woman, barely of age, submissively kneeling in front of you, big doe eyes looking up for approval as she sucks your cock.

But that's not how it'll happen with a people-pleaser, who tend to attract narcissists such as hobbyists. People-pleasers have grown up equating intrinsic lovability with usefulness to others. Calling oneself a people-pleaser in your escort ad will instinctively attract the self-absorbed, thoughtless, and exploitative client looking for a transaction with a provider whose brand promise is to push aside her own emotional needs in exchange for money and her drugs of choice. She will become precisely what her client needs her to be, which can only lead to codependency, which enables the controlling self-obsession and insensitivity that all hobbyists bring to the table.

If you're nice enough, or mean enough, and you pay her upfront, Kaylee might go down on you. To be clear, she's not doing it to please you. Technically, yes, she will be pleasuring you. But the act of giving pleasure is how she controls the situation. When she assumes the position of maestro orchestrating the symphony of the people in her life, especially the ones she may never see again, that's the only time she feels safe. She'll quell any of her real feelings in an attempt to empathize with your mood. Giving you what you desire to control you is her top priority. She knows what you need, a much more fundamental drive than what you think you want. So, she gives you what she knows is best because clients can't take care of themselves, and it's her duty to save them from themselves.

People-pleasers' subconscious penchant for constantly putting aside their own needs and responding to what others require ultimately leads to rage and resentment, seeking an escape valve. People pleasing can make the pleaser feel overlooked, taken for granted, and burned out. Sometimes, the anger and resentment can manifest in an explosive outburst or turn inward and become masochistic. Often, this resentment can manifest in a passive-aggressive behavior that turns people-pleasers into the very narcissists that they were raised to please, which is their way of defending themselves. In turn, the exploitative clients become the exploited, many of whom find that they are inexplicably drawn to their new dominatrix.

Whenever Kaylee sensed her dates' vulnerability, she'd act cold and a little mean, perhaps even climbing out the bathroom window while they lay in bed, only in their boxers, waiting for her to return. But after five minutes or so, Kaylee's protector, a tall black dude named Isaac with a very civilized manner (and not her pimp because he doesn't take her money, though she does support him) comes out from the other room to introduce himself, gets a soda from the refrigerator, and announces that Kaylee has already left. She'll take your money and the drugs that were included as part of the payment, and leave you stranded.

That's what she did to me the first time we met, and I knew I had to see her again.

As I was driving to the motel in Kent to meet Kaylee for the first time, I intended to use her. She was half my age. If she was selling herself, I figured she couldn't have been educated. That meant I was better than her. But all I really wanted was for her to like me in the way that escorts won't allow themselves to like their clients. Then, I'd feel like I had won the prize of her affection and admiration. I wanted to break down the emotional barriers that call girls erect to maintain professionalism.

I wanted nothing to do with that level of professionalism. It's overrated. I mean, I had built a career in which I literally helped build the internet into what it is today—a worldwide oversexed, overspent, insecure, and manipulative public space that feeds off our collective addictions. I've worked in offices in Edinburgh, London, Paris, Beijing, Taipei, San Francisco, Silicon Valley, San Diego, Portland, and Seattle. I was trained to be professional. But human behavior cannot avoid becoming mired in its damp messiness. The game I played with women of the night who had honed the skill of emotional distance forced upon them from childhood trauma into a studied expertise was to use my looks, charm, charisma, and access to money and drugs to make them fall for me. The planning ended there. I had no idea what I'd do once the veil was lifted.

The allure of a clean transaction with a dirty girl may have been the initial attraction, but what I wanted was a deep connection, and I didn't know it.

I honed my skills of catching top-shelf escorts during the Craigslist Casual Encounters era of the mid-2000s. After my divorce, I didn't want to lose myself in another person, which had been my modus operandi: meet a woman in the upper echelon of physical beauty; charm the pants off her; fall head over heels for each other; within a month move in with her or have her move in with me...whichever one of us had a better apartment; wake up a month later after she had lifted her veil and I had let down my guard, and have no idea why this person had all their stuff in my place, or I was stuck at her place; continue hanging on for dear life and to the bitter end because I felt like I would die without her; rinse and repeat. After my divorce, I intended to eschew any level of relationship that required me to lose myself in another person for any length of time.

That description was my only definition of Love. I didn't know any better. No one had shown me any other way. I got on Match.com at first. I made my profile and reached out to women whose profiles tickled my fancy. But I must have come across as too deep, contrived, narcissistic, or worst of all, desperate because I got no responses.

Then one night, I finally summoned the courage to answer a Craigslist Casual Encounters personal ad. I wrote a witty line, attached a photo of myself wearing sunglasses while lighting a cigarette with the Santa Monica beach in the background. New to the scene, I didn't have the savvy in the Casual Encounters game to know that any woman who posted there received hundreds of emails, especially the posts with no photos attached, because those are often the quality ones. The supply of real women was a koi pond compared to the ocean of demand filled with horny sharks. My first hit came surprisingly quickly, and the effect was exactly like a person with the genetic predisposition to addiction winning at the casino for the first time. I was hooked.

The online call girl trade is one industry in which inflation has had no impact. For nearly 20 years, the asking price for a nice-looking woman has remained around $300 on escort sites. It's free to list your sex services on these sites. If a lady of the night wanted to charge a premium, she needed to pay to play on premium escort sites. The nicest women didn't call out their prices. You had to know that your starting point to negotiate fees would be $200, or you weren't ready for quality.

Cheap dudes trawled these sites hoping to engage a potential one-night date who was dope sick and out of money to get her fix. He might have a bag of heroin to trade straight across for sex, which meant a trade value of $40 since any guy holding a spare bag got his heroin in bulk. Or Mr. Cheap Ass could read the dope-sick desperation in between the lines of the multitude of texts exchanged during the hours-long courting period and take advantage by negotiating a sub-$100 price. Then there are the guys who offer the $300 upfront to show how flush they are and impress their tawdry target. These guys obliviously set themselves up as marks.

When Mr. Mark arrives at the hotel door, the experienced sex worker will answer the door naked to throw him off, take the money, and then delay gratification to extract more money.

It took Kaylee a few hours to text back.

ME: "It's about time."

KAYLEE: "Lol…I just woke up."

ME: "You wanna get fucked up?"

This closing line was my standard proposition. It immediately filtered out the escorts who preferred not to get high with their clients. They weren't any fun in my book. Plus, I couldn't prepare a package of cash plus narcotics that would allow me to use whatever paltry sum of money I had left from giving away and mismanaging my tech executive salary to cover my habit and hobby. Moreover, I immediately inserted 'fuck' into the conversation while avoiding outright rudeness.

KAYLEE: "Ya."

ME: "That's me."

I sent my LinkedIn profile to show her my financial legitimacy with a dashing headshot as the cherry on top. There is always a slightly longer pause at this point in the negotiation. She can't seem too eager.

KAYLEE: "What were you thinking?"

ME: "$200 and a nice shard…it's about an eighth."

To support my meth habit, I would buy an ounce every payday, deliver three-quarters to three established middle-aged guys whom I had met in various business settings—they all appreciated my clean-cut appearance and discretion. I charged enough to cover the entire cost of the original investment and retained a quarter for myself for the trouble.

Giving away an eighth as part of Kaylee's compensation package was a much smaller sliver of skin off my nose than cash.

KAYLEE: "I'll text you in an hour with directions, hun."

Just like that.

The city of Kent is about 10 miles southeast of Seattle. It's an industrial area frayed at the edges that was once the startup capital of the Northwest when Boeing was the big deal—the aircraft company's size and influence created a gravitational pull around which upstart airplane parts suppliers were attracted, revolved, and grew. Well before Microsoft or Amazon established the tech scene, Kent was the locus of the aviation scene. When Kaylee was living homelessly there, its claim to fame was a concentrated row of motels infamous for trapping (drug dealing) and tricking (prostitution).

I didn't have a clue during my inaugural visit. All I knew was that I had to make it to the last ferry leaving Bainbridge Island for downtown Seattle—a 35-minute sailing across the Puget Sound—otherwise, I would have had to make the long drive around the Puget Sound, through Bremerton, over to Tacoma, and up to Kent. I made it on the last ferry sailing, drove through the bright lights of downtown Seattle, and headed south on I-5 toward the industrial shade of south King County.

In its heyday, these types of motels were where highway travelers would stop for a long rest, as if it were a holiday home. The unit Kaylee stayed in was surprisingly spacious, with a kitchenette, sitting area, bedroom, and bathroom. But the room, like the property, was dingy and unkempt. The proprietors were Indian Asians. Their target market was the hidden homeless: transients with no tangible work history, rental history, or ID. They would charge daily rates rivaling those of downtown motels—and monthly rates equal to a two-bedroom apartment in a decent neighborhood—for roach-infested rooms, because no one else would accept the undocumented past of their target market. Part of me was excited to be in such stereotypical squalor. The other part looked down my nose at how the other half lived. I secretly felt I was doing Kaylee a favor just by my presence.

At the same time, I just hoped she liked me.

***

It did not end well between Kaylee and me.

How could it have ended any other way than with me, the police, and casino security waiting for her to exit the casino, about a 20-minute drive from where I had shacked up for two months with her and Isaac? I was still a cop caller—getting help from the police remained a last resort, as I maintained a connection to the establishment. At the end of my two-month introduction to the underground, Kaylee, Isaac, and I were in transition, having been kicked out of the Kent motel because Kaylee had gone on one of her gambling binges, wagering away all the money she made hooking, as well as the cash I had given her to manage as house money (yeah, I thought giving her that money instead of directly paying a week's motel rent would prove my trust in her and make her like me more).

After leaving Kent, I secured a motel room by the airport, using points I had left when I used to travel for business, but Kaylee and Isaac never showed up—they ran off with my car, leaving me waiting for them in the room that I had thought would be our next shared trap of domestic bliss.

Kaylee had been setting me up the whole time. I was what they call a "mark"—someone just asking to be duped and violated.

"Be careful, man. You're a mark," Isaac told me one night when Kaylee had left us in the room together.

I thought that all I needed was to hear that warning once, and I could remain vigilant enough of my marked behavior to avoid being seen and treated as such. I figured that my dark Filipino complexion and predilection for meth would override the suburban naivete that I brought to the scene. Never mind that I drove a brand-new car, dressed in mid-level designer brands, spoke with precise grammar, and still had clear skin.

I was giddy with excitement the night that Kaylee finally let me stay with her and Isaac in the motel room where I would envision dark dealings going down while sitting in the parking lot night after night, waiting for her to text "wya" (where you at), to give me a little sign that she cared about my well-being. But I tried to be cool about the invitation to shack up with them. Earlier that fateful night, I had rented a room at a three-star hotel, right next door to Kaylee's motel, and had been texting up a storm with her. I was wielding words in my way to entice her to be with me, offering to increase her business with my marketing savvy while providing back-up funds when she just needed a day off. I wanted her to take days off so I could have her to myself.

I was a much better option than Isaac. I wasn't nearly as physically imposing, but overall, I was the more secure bet.

Kaylee relented and asked to borrow my car to see how far she could push my boundaries.

I had purchased my new car at the advice of my bankruptcy lawyer—he said I should buy a decent car before entering bankruptcy because your vehicle is one of the possessions the bankruptcy trust won't confiscate, and I needed something dependable and efficient to get me through the five years of the agreement. That car would become a motif of the codependency that drove my descent into the streets:

- Denial—perceiving myself as completely unselfish and devoted to the well-being of others; willfully ignoring the unavailability of people to whom I was attracted
- Low Self-Esteem—regarding others' approval of my thinking, feelings, and behavior over my own; perceiving myself as superior; unable to set healthy priorities and boundaries
- Compliance—loyal to the point of endangering myself; placing others' interests above my own; accepting sexual attention in place of love.

I drove across the street to our parking lot, gave Kaylee the keys, and slouched back to my more expensive hotel room.

At the time, I was still paying for my car's monthly GPS tracking subscription, which I had to use the next night when Kaylee didn't show up as promised after I had checked out of the hotel, hung around the lobby until I felt uncomfortable about loitering as a non-paying customer, ate at a 24-hour diner down the street, and sat in the booth until the same non-paying discomfort became overwhelming, all the while Kaylee ghosting my texts.

Finally, I did what I didn't want—use the GPS tracking app on my phone to pinpoint my car's whereabouts: the casino. I didn't want to resort to tracking her down because it would mean she was using me. Nah, she was playing a coy little game with me, that's all. I booked an Uber to the casino, used the GPS app to flash my car's parking lights and unlock the doors, climbed in, and waited for her to come out. About half an hour later, Kaylee arrived with Isaac in tow.

"How'd he do that?" Isaac was pissed off.

Kaylee looked unsurprised. She handed me the keys and I drove us back to our motel.

When I pulled in, I stayed in the car.

Kaylee got out, turned around, and leaned in.

"You coming?"

I slowly exited the car with as much nonchalance as I could muster, got my duffle bag, and followed them into the room.

Kaylee pointed to the same bed where she had abandoned me the first night we met.

"That's yours."

During my two-month stint in Kent, I shared my car with Kaylee. She would go out on her nightly escapades, usually returning mid-afternoon the next day or at dawn two days later and promptly heading to the front desk to pay for our room. I was still working my corporate job, where I had been given a new role, focusing more on strategy, which meant I was being paid for my ideas. I had also been given freer rein over my schedule, meaning I could "work from home" as I saw fit. Good thing, since most of the time, Kaylee wouldn't return to the room in time for me to get to work during those fleeting moments when I felt guilty about being out of the office for so long.

Sometimes, not often, Kaylee's dates came to the motel. That's when Isaac and I would be on guard duty—we would drive to the closest parking lot, sit there with our phones ready, and wait for Kaylee to text us. One time, we decided to stay in the parking lot of our motel, but two dark guys sitting in a car spooked one of her visiting clients. He berated Kaylee for having her goons waiting in the car, cut the date short, and drove off.

After that incident, she demanded that we stay away from our motel but remain close enough to reach her quickly, if needed. There was only one time that Isaac and I had to save her from a date—he had creeped her out instantly, so she texted us; all we had to do was perform a "police knock" on the door, and the guy hurried out. Waiting in a parked car for Kaylee made me feel like her savior and abuser all wrapped up in a package of jumbled emotions and excitement. I never wanted even to approach the notion of being her abuser—she'd had enough to last two lifetimes.

During one of the few nights when all three of us were in the motel room together and had enough of our respective drugs of choice to get satisfactorily high, I could easily overhear Kaylee and Isaac talking, and they knew it. She was recounting the story of her first high-school boyfriend trying to have sex with her. They had talked about it before, but she told him she was a virgin, so he waited. Kaylee believed that she was a virgin. But when her first boyfriend finally tried it on, she froze, and her buried memories erupted. Her prostitute mother had sent her to live with her aunt, who was a lawyer, because her mother thought that living with her put-together aunt would protect Kaylee from a sordid life. However, the entire time Kaylee lived with her aunt in a polite neighborhood, her aunt's son, Kaylee's older and much bigger cousin, ritually raped her every single night.

"The things he made me do," Kaylee exclaimed in a hushed tone.

This went on for years until her cousin was sent to prison. Life was peaceful then. But one day, Kaylee heard her cousin's voice in the house—he had returned from prison. She ran away that very night. And that's how she inherited the family business. Sometimes during our sojourn together, Kaylee would return to the room and tell me and Isaac how she ran into her mother on Hilltop, a Tacoma neighborhood renowned for drugs and hustling.

"She's still getting business," Kaylee would say, her voice saturated with utter sadness belied by a bit of pride.

Most of the time, Isaac and I would be stuck in the room together, wondering where Kaylee was, who she was with, when would she get back, was she gambling the room money, would we get kicked out by motel management because we hadn't paid for the room for a few days? At those desperate times, I wished I hadn't canceled the GPS subscription in an explicit attempt to show Kaylee my implicit trust in her. Around the same time, she told me that she had lost the key fob I had given her to use, so whenever she took the car out, she used the only remaining key fob.

The day Kaylee, Isaac, and I were evicted from our motel, my desperate questions were answered affirmatively. For a week straight, Kaylee had gambled away all the paper she had chased every night and the house money I had given her. I made a lot of money then, but I never had any. For my entire life, I never learned and didn't want to know how to manage my money. My financial plan revolved around making more money. But the more I made, the more I spent on clothes, shoes, dining in restaurants and ordering take-out every day, going to bars during the week and clubs every weekend, personal travel during business trips, providing financial support to others who were sufficiently grown to provide for themselves, and, most of all, a constant stream of drugs and hookers.

After Kaylee and Isaac abandoned me, I had nowhere to go but back to Bainbridge Island. I returned to an empty house—my dog of sixteen years, Bridget, had died a few years before my foray into the underground. I had kicked out my roommate after a massive argument—he was a dog walker and had moved in to look after Bridget while I was at work and ease the financial burden of my mortgage. With Bridget dead, our differences came to the fore. He turned out to be an alcoholic, while I secretly took stimulants every night. We had absolutely nothing in common.

I did not want to be in that house.

For two months, I took the bus from my house to the ferry terminal, sailed across the Puget Sound to downtown Seattle, walked four blocks rain or shine to the bus stop where the Bellevue-Factoria bus picked me up and took me across the I-90 Lake Washington floating bridge to my office—a three-hour commute. Fortunately, I was allowed to work from home at least three days per week. Sometimes, I wouldn't go into the office all week. I felt like a fool, like I deserved what I got, deserved to take the bus to my company's technology complex surrounded by posh neighborhoods, deserved to put up a façade and pretend that I was still a respectable technology worker living in a leafy neighborhood and had made a conscious decision to commute for three hours.

I felt even more of an imposter than I did at any time during my career. I was 52 years old and still just a senior manager, passed over for director and vice president positions in a global technology company because I had never prioritized getting an MBA. The only jobs in which I had the title that I thought I deserved were in small startups, but those titles didn't translate to large companies. I had no savings or investments and was staring at a looming retirement on government benefits. But I didn't even know how to make ends meet on a tech worker's salary and annual bonus, so there'd be no way I could survive on social security.

The only thing that assuaged the overwhelming impostor syndrome every time I got near the office building—sneaking into a Starbucks private restroom to snort a line of meth—was the coolness of my double life.

The story I told myself was that every middle-aged director or vice president at my office would kill to have my exciting life on the down low.

But here I was, stranded, bus-bound, and taken by a 22-year-old hooker.

On weekends, I would rent a car and trawl the casinos in Auburn, Fife, and Tacoma, looking for my car. One night, while sitting in a rental car in one of the casino parking lots, I saw Isaac drive out of the lot in my car. I was so surprised that I instinctively called the police—while living with Kaylee and Isaac, I had been trained not to trust the police anymore, but Isaac was bigger than me, I didn't have a gun, and I wasn't trying to get into a car chase. The police officer arrived, and I told him an abbreviated version of my story.

"I'm sorry, Mr. Leyva, but there's not much we can do right now. You gave her the keys. This is more of a civil matter. If there's any way you can catch the car parked somewhere in Auburn, call me, and we should be able to do something." He handed me his card.

Throughout my two-month abandonment after the car heist that I had permitted, I would often text Kaylee and demand that she give up the phone line I had given her on our second night together, along with a string of phones that she kept losing (selling), because I didn't want her to continue benefitting off my resources.

Kaylee continued to ghost me and kept using the line. Then one day, it occurred to me: I have access and complete control over every phone line on my account. I researched what would happen if I wanted to tap into Kaylee's line. I had to select her line on my carrier's app and have her texts routed to my app in parallel; texts would still appear on her phone simultaneously. But there was a catch—requesting parallel routing would trigger a notification to her phone. So, I called customer service and told them I did not want this notification sent. They complied. No questions asked.

I eavesdropped on Kaylee's texts for two weeks while devising a plan.

On the night things ended badly, I'd been on a four-day meth binge. I picked up yet another rental car I had booked the day before. I scanned Kaylee's line as she texted her cronies about plans to be at a casino that night. So, I drove to Auburn while she told her crew she was on her way. I only had to drive around the parking lot for a minute before spotting my car—she had found a prime parking spot steps from the main entrance. I pulled up behind my long-lost car to block it, pulled out the policeman's business card, and called him.

Casino security paged Kaylee to please meet them at "her" car. She exited the casino through a side door and walked as disinterestedly as possible to our conspicuous gathering, keeping her gaze on her phone, while Isaac trailed far behind her. When she finally approached, the policeman ordered her to give me back my keys.

"But he gave me the car."

"No. I didn't."

With all eyes on her—the police officer, a gang of casino security, and nosy passers-by—Kaylee relented quickly.

"I can't drive two cars," I told the officer.

He calmed me down, "Just move your car and park the rental in that spot. I'll call the rental agency and inform them of what happened. They'll pick up their own car. Just leave the keys with me."

I was so grateful.

As I drove away, Kaylee texted.

KAYLEE: "Can you drop me off at my date?"

I didn't answer. I was livid at the thought that she assumed I'd fall for her ruse…again. Instead, I drove to the Goodwill down the hill and donated all her possessions, which were packed to the brim in the hatchback. Every single thing she owned.

"There's some cool stuff in here." The woman at the donation station admired the items I pulled out of my car.

Kaylee, Isaac, and I were not a love triangle. None of us knew anything about love. We created a trauma bond triangle, rotating the roles of abuser and victim amongst the three of us. All any of us ever knew was trauma bonding, alternating kindness and cruelty whenever it allowed one to gain the advantage over the others. We isolated one another, became dependent on each other, forging a bond with the potency to make us loyal to each other's abuse.

As I drove away from the Goodwill where I finally jettisoned Kaylee from my car, I pulled into an empty lot and wept. I woke up and saw on the dashboard clock that I'd been asleep for five hours. The gas gauge showed one-quarter less gas in the tank. The engine had been running the whole time.

* * *

Six years later, on Thanksgiving Day, five months after my social service startup launched full-time operations, Isaac contacted me on LinkedIn. He was one of only two people from the underground with a LinkedIn profile—he understood how to present a buttoned-up image.

- Nov 28, 2024 -

ISAAC: "Hey. Do u still use this?"

ME: "Happy Thanksgiving, man ."

ISAAC: "Happy Thanksgiving! I don't know any other way to get a hold of you, but I could really use some assistance in life.... Like, seriously, I'm reaching out right now because I'm about to be outside with nowhere to go, no way to make any money, and I don't wanna fall by the wayside. I was staying in my car, but it got impounded with everything I owned...I just need a break frfr cause I'm like this close to giving up.... I read your LinkedIn and figured I'd hit you up and see if there is ANY kind of assistance I can take advantage of?"

ME: "This is how I might be able to help (link to www.homeycorps.com). You gotta get to a detox first..."

ISAAC: "Well, I'm not too sure if I qualify all the way cuz I haven't done any drugs other than weed in like almost a year, and I'm not in any trouble with the law."

ME: "You're off street drugs?"

ISAAC: "Yeah, just being honest with you, cuz we have history, and you know my potential to do anything I put my mind to…I'm really trying to be preemptive."

ME: "But we both know you've been in jail before and on loads of drugs. Weed counts, too."

ISAAC: "Yes, and if you're counting weed then ok great, but I don't know if me giving up weed is all that high on the list of things that may hinder my progress."

ME: "I need to talk with my business partner and the owner of the recovery house where we place our clients, but you'd have to give up weed. I'm offering you a golden ticket. It comes with restrictions. Think about it."

ISAAC: "Look, I'm not tryna argue at all so please don't take what I'm saying as argumentative cause that's not my intent…If I gotta give up weed for a roof over my head so I can have the stability in order to do the things I need to have a future I guess I gotta quit smoking weed then. I just need to get in asap. I am squatting."

ME: "Ok. Understand that if we can work this out, the house has a zero-tolerance policy, so if you get caught using any substances whatsoever, you're out. We also require you to attend addiction outpatient and mental health services. And you gotta play on our sober softball team next season. This won't happen today. This will take a thoughtful process from both of us."

ISAAC: "Ok, although idk how well I'd do at softball. I don't have complete use of my hands cause of a robbery attempt in 2022. I had to fight a guy with a machete and ended up with 16 stitches and lost the use of two fingers on both hands. But I'd be willing to make a fool of myself trying."

ME: "I've made a fool of myself for two years because I didn't grow up playing baseball. I'm finally getting good."

ISAAC: "So, where do I sign up, or what hoops do I gotta jump through?"

ME: "Just got in touch with the recovery residence owner. The house is full. But things change quickly, so I want to keep in touch. I always thought of you when I was creating my agency. You're the profile of the type of people we want to grow our organization. You are among the smartest people I know, at any level and context."

ISAAC: "Well, it seems like things happen for a reason. Let's get the ball rolling."

ME: "It's already rolling. We are waiting for a vacancy at the recovery house. Things can turn quickly in a place like that—people relapse or move out suddenly—but it may take longer than you'd like. Trust in the universe."

- Dec 1, 2024 -

ISAAC: "Well, I'm officially outside with nowhere to go and no legal income…I'm trying not to go back into the life of drugs and prostitution, and it's not looking too good."

ME: "Here's the sad truth—if you do that, then I can get you into detox, then you can stay off the streets longer in a 28-day intensive inpatient treatment program, and by that time, a spot at the recovery house might open up. But would you be in the frame of mind to want to quit the life?"

ISAAC: "Yeah, I don't think that is the route I'm gonna take…I guess I will just wait for an opening."

ME: "I'm also going to talk with the inpatient facility where I used to work and see if they will take someone into their program who's been on street drugs before but only does weed now, if you're willing."

ISAAC: "I can do some meth right now if it can get me into some housing faster. Never thought that not doing drugs would hinder me from finding housing… and it's cold out here, so I guess I'm about to smoke some right now, then."

ME: "That's the sad truth. You're on Medicaid. Right?"

ISAAC: "I gotta re-sign back up. I wish there was some kinda funding for me to get a room…I'm not cut out for this homelessness outside…what's your number?"

ME: "More sad truth, and then I gotta sleep. If you get high right now, then you can go to the ER and they'll sign you up for Medicaid again, and then they'll place you in detox. Ask them to call the facility where I used to work. Tell them you've been talking to me about Homey Corps. But I'm not giving you my number yet because I have to maintain healthy boundaries."

I haven't heard from Isaac since.

Chapter 3

Suburban Underground

I'm not looking forward to writing this chapter. I don't want to write it. It's not Ava's fault. I've processed my experience with her. I was given the chance to make my amends with her before she died suddenly, so I'm at peace with Ava. It's my ex-wife that I don't want to talk about. I've avoided discussing her throughout the Introduction and the first two chapters. But I can't dodge it any longer. To speak about Ava, I need to talk about my ex-wife. I inserted Ava between me and my ex-wife, eventually sabotaging my lifestyle so that I had nothing left to give to either of them. That way, I wouldn't be forced to say the one word that would have liberated me from my self-destructive behaviors: No.

My ex-wife was living in my house on Bainbridge Island during my time with Kaylee—I didn't want to live with her, so I found a way to stay elsewhere and have my drugs within easy access. My ex-wife found that house for me—it was the only one in the entire island that I could afford...well, that I could portray myself as being able to afford if I didn't include the non-court-ordered but legally contractual payments that I was making to my ex-wife in the mortgage application. She and I had made plans to share the property as a retirement house, one of us staying there while the other was away. But when I told her I had discounted her monthly stipend from my income on the mortgage application, she pulled out of our deal on the house.

The house felt like an albatross. I eventually stopped paying the mortgage because I understood the complexity and length of the eviction process, so I used it to my advantage. My ex-wife offered to take the property off my hands by assuming the mortgage payments, as usual, I didn't tell her the whole story behind the mortgage arrears, so she moved in, promising to pay the mortgage once I'd moved out. When she discovered that I hadn't paid the mortgage for months, she followed suit, so I told her to move out, but only after weeks of stewing about it before I could muster the courage to take something back that I didn't want. But even after all that, I resentfully continued paying her monthly stipend, which equaled the lion's share of my take-home pay, to pay a debt I incurred when my actions (or inaction) caused her to lose her house in Los Angeles.

That's a microcosm of the corrosive dynamic between us, which was a significant driver of my descent—blowing up my past life once and for all was the only way I could escape the oppressive obligations created by the porous boundaries of a spineless heap of flesh clinically referred to as a codependent. I didn't know how to say no. At least, that's how I see it now, but at the time, I was merely running on impulse without the self-awareness that comes with developing the capability to engage my prefrontal cortex. I don't want the contents of my memoir to drive my ex-wife on a rampage, which is the effect that much of my past behavior had on her. I want to be fair and truthful, providing only enough information to further this story.

What I need to do, then, is provide a testimony just as I had done in Step 1 of MRT (Moral Reconation Therapy) during my time in Phase 1 of the Drug Court program.

MRT is the standard behavioral treatment program for justice system-involved people with substance use and co-occurring disorders. The term "moral" doesn't merely connote the traditional sense of the word but rather denotes a higher level of cognitive reasoning. "Reconation" is manufactured from the psychological term "conation," meaning the process of formulating conscious decisions.

MRT promotes better decision-making and appropriate behavior in people with underdeveloped attachment styles because, as children, their caregivers didn't know how to give them enough attention and affection to find security in the world. MRT is designed to amend the anti-social behaviors that have turned into self-destructive survival skills. The program follows a 12-step structure, so it's familiar to people new in recovery exposed to 12-step fellowships. Drug Court participants are usually required to start MRT within the first two phases of the program.

MRT Step 1 always trips people up, requiring participants to give objective testimony. The exact meaning of this act eludes most people, especially those whose brains are in the process of healing after a lifetime of externally imposed and self-inflicted trauma. The Oxford Dictionary defines it as "a formal written or spoken statement, especially one given in a court of law." The MRT instructor instructs participants to explain the things they did that harmed others. But what happens with addicts full of themselves, who affect an air of superiority but feel utterly inferior, is that they turn the testimony into a bragging festival, full of war stories, and insert a small, perfunctory helping of contrition for the wake of destruction that their past lives had become. Ultimately, they can't help themselves from ladling a heaping helping of blame and justification. It took me four tries to surmount the obstacle of MRT Step 1.

The trick, I discovered, is two-pronged: 1) Recount the relevant actions and their repercussions; 2) Stop being a dick. So, that's my intention, not just for the first part of this chapter, but also for the entire book. However, the MRT Step 1 instructions also forbid including your emotions in the testimony. Sorry, but emotions cannot be excluded from a memoir.

I met my ex-wife in Scotland. We were part of the clubbing-and-drugging crew, which inducted me into the Order of the Professional Drug Addicts. When my ex-wife would recount how she was mercilessly bullied in childhood, yet her parents wouldn't (they said they couldn't) do much about it, the combination of her beauty and trauma incited my savior complex kicked in like never before. She wanted to live in the U.S., so after two years working for a software localization agency in Edinburgh, I applied and accepted a job offer with Adobe in San Jose, CA. I wanted to live in cool San Francisco, and so did she. But the continued drug-taking and excessively long commute took its toll—I couldn't afford that lifestyle and the Bay Area's notoriously high cost of living for both of us on my entry-level tech income.

My ex-wife moved back to Scotland. Alone and missing her, I moped and continued doing coke and ecstasy. I racked up a huge phone bill by calling her from my office phone every day, even if she didn't want to talk (these were the days before messaging apps). I persuaded her to return to the States on a fiancée visa, which seemed the only way. We got married in Las Vegas and honeymooned in New Orleans during Mardi Gras, either taking drugs or looking for them the whole time. I continued to mismanage the money and wouldn't let her touch it. I secretly kept doing drugs, switching exclusively to cocaine. She quit hard drugs and settled on weed, which she could do openly, as it is socially acceptable compared to my drugs of choice.

We moved to Los Angeles, but after a couple of years, she had had enough of a life of constant teetering on the brink of financial ruin and filed for divorce. We never had kids. I started paying her alimony, which continued for 10 years. She grew that money with astute real estate investments during the heydays of cheap interest rates before the Financial Crisis of the late-2000s.

Whenever I would run out of money, which my drug use and newfound prostitute addiction made a regular occurrence, I would leverage the continuation of the alimony as financial domination, staying at her place and eating her food or demanding (pleading) for money.

When the Financial Crisis hit in 2008, she planned on selling her house while she still had the chance, but I told her that I'd buy it, knowing full well that I didn't have the credit score or down payment to do so. I moved in with her just as the bottom fell out of the real estate market. After a year of unemployment for me, and her usual part-time work was never enough to support her, we were evicted from her house.

For about a month, we lived in motels on the money she had put away for a rainy day. Then I got lucky and landed a job in San Diego, making as much money as I had before unemployment. We found a place one block from the beach in Carlsbad. She stayed with me but eventually moved back to Scotland after her beloved dog died. A year later, I visited her in Scotland and had a great time, so I invited her back to San Diego, hoping she would take the alimony money I had saved for her and jump-start a new life...without me.

Within weeks of her return, Microsoft offered me a job and a relocation package to move to Bellevue. I asked my ex-wife to return with me, inserting her as a buffer between me and my family, to whom I had been estranged ever since I moved to Scotland. My ex-wife and I signed an agreement that, within six years, I would pay her back the full purchase price of the Los Angeles house that my actions had caused her to lose. I eventually paid back 93% of that until I moved Ava into the Bainbridge Island house.

I've skipped over a lot. Including everything would take an entire book of its own. What I have included in this testimony indicates what psychologist Robert Sternberg calls Empty Love—commitment (or loyalty) without physical and emotional intimacy. Sometimes, an intense love (which I once had for my ex-wife) deteriorates into empty love. She and I still had passion, but it was rechanneled toward our frequent all-out fights. I did not want to be with her, nor was I physically attracted to her, after our divorce. But I felt that it was my responsibility to support her because, as fiercely independent as she was, she couldn't support herself without me. This misplaced belief imprisoned me in resentment and hopelessness. I would turn to drugs and prostitutes for relief.

The first time I recounted this tale in testimony form—without demonizing my ex-wife or reflexively defending her behavior as a way of reluctantly shouldering the blame—was to my first Drug Court counselor, Carol. She would serve as my counselor for only one month, but she became my mentor throughout my time in Drug Court. She was a card-carrying codependent in recovery, so she saw straight away the hell that I had fashioned for myself.

"I haven't touched alcohol in decades, but I relapse into codependency every day. It is your source addiction, too. If you can learn to manage your codependency, you can stay clean," my mentor said before telling me the story of the codependent caterpillar…

A child found a chrysalis staring in amazement at the nascent butterfly flapping its new, unformed wings, struggling to find its way out. Wanting to help, the child peeled back the layers of the chrysalis, freeing the thing inside. What came out was no longer a caterpillar or a fully formed butterfly. The thing couldn't fly, but it couldn't walk either. The child didn't understand the necessity of the would-be butterfly's struggle to gain the strength to fly independently. The chrysalis' struggle is a gift—a requirement to become what the butterfly is meant to be. By peeling away the struggle, the child was left with an unformed, dependent half-thing.

I created and perpetuated my ex-wife's dependence. She may have called it my responsibility or debt. But it was dependence by another name.

It would take years of recovery before I knew how to set healthy boundaries—entailing MRT, drug counseling, mental health therapy, two stints in inpatient addiction treatment facilities, and memberships in multiple 12-Step fellowships—so when my ex-wife tried on a piece of emotional blackmail that became the final straw, I set unhealthy boundaries by subconsciously deciding to sabotage my untenable lifestyle completely.

I had been with Ava for a couple of weeks when my ex-wife decided to fly back to the U.S. for a visit. Of course, I offered her the Bainbridge house to stay in. I stayed with Ava in a room she rented in a trailer home near Suquamish. Ava didn't understand why I would leave with no place to stay just because my ex-wife was visiting. I didn't explain.

The day before my ex-wife's departure, I returned to the Bainbridge house to get a few things. She showed off how she had cleaned, tidied, and rearranged the place to make it more feng shui. I appreciated what she had done—she was good at interior decorating. In my head, I'd been counting down the final four stipend-debt payments. She brought up the subject, painting a picture of having difficulty finding work that could support her, and how I knew from my character defects just how controlling guys can be when they're with a woman without means. If I could continue giving her a stipend, smaller than the payments I'd been making, she wouldn't fall prey to such unscrupulous men.

I didn't know what to say. My chance at freedom, only four months away, collapsed. Even at the lowest points I would experience when I eventually descended to the streets as a homeless criminal drug addict, I have never before or since felt the hopelessness that descended upon me during that conversation. I reflexively, reluctantly nodded and left the house as fast as possible, waiting until she'd gone before returning.

* * *

Ava was the last straw that broke my lifestyle apart. Yet, I look back on her and our time fondly. Not only because I managed to make my amends to her six months before she died in a car accident about a quarter mile from her parents' house on the cusp of Poulsbo and Suquamish, but also because we got to spend a little time getting reacquainted (or should I say, actually acquainted) years after all the shit between us blew up. Ava got to witness the earnest beginnings of my ascent.

Ava got me higher than I had ever felt in my life. I fell for her because she was the first person to shoot me up with meth successfully. After that, I let her get away with anything.

After I got my car back from Kaylee and before meeting Ava, I met a woman on MeetMe. I spent my time driving back and forth to Aberdeen, birthplace of Kurt Cobain, where this woman lived with her parents after years of living off guys. We stayed in motels or casinos when I visited. She wanted to take my intravenous-drug-use virginity, as I had never shot up drugs before. She always had guys shoot her up, so she didn't know how to do it for herself, let alone someone else. That strategy allowed her to avoid seeing herself as an outright IV user, though there was always some guy around who would gladly accommodate her. I borrowed her strategy during my entire IV-use career.

One of my middle-aged meth customers was an exclusive IV user, so the three of us planned a little shot party, during which he would shoot us both up—me for the first time. Surprisingly, the shot didn't affect me much, which disappointed me. It was so much more than a disappointment for my Aberdeen girl—we disintegrated shortly afterwards. I found Ava online about a week later.

"Can you hit me?" I knew this question would seal the deal with the right person.

"Ya. Black or clear?" ("Black" is the street name for heroin and "clear" for meth.)

I had just driven an hour from the rest area just north of Fife on I-5—where I would sleep sometimes when I had barely enough money to hire a hooker but not enough for a motel room—to Suquamish, looking for something to do. Turns out that something would be Ava.

She was staying at an infamous motel on Kitsap Way in Bremerton, a rundown, notorious hangout for the liminal homeless—prostitutes, drug dealers, and their hangers-on. Ava stayed in one of the suites, answering the door and leading me past the living area to the back room. It was the first time I saw her youngest son, who would live with me, his mother, and older brother in my house for six months. He was lying on the sofa, watching television while drinking from his bottle. Our eyes met as I walked past, and he quickly shifted his gaze back to the TV, frantically sucking on his bottle, his go-to soothing mechanism.

Ava expertly mixed a shot up for me—packing tiny meth kernels into the barrel, delicately reinserting the plunger to push the meth kernels down, placing the needle into a small container filled with spring water from a bottle, slowly drawing the plunger up to pull water into the barrel, then wafting her lighter's flame across the barrel to kickstart the liquefication process of the meth kernels in the water, and finally rolling the barrel back and forth between her palms several times to create sufficient friction heat to complete the liquefication. I rolled up my sleeve.

Ava took the scarf off her long brown hair and tied it around my upper arm. I still had the veins of a recent IV virgin, so she easily found a suitable vein at the crook of my inner arm. She inserted the needle with slow confidence, blowing air from her puckered lips as she did so. She pulled the plunger back ever so slightly to register a tiny bit of blood into the barrel, confirming that the needle was in my vein. Then she pushed the plunger down elegantly.

The effect was immediate. I was hers.

"You got great legs." I stared at Ava's bare legs.

She looked away shyly, surprised at how much my heartfelt candor affected her. From that day forward, getting shot up with meth acted as a truth serum on me. Our first time together, we had unprotected sex. After our interlude, as I was driving back to Bainbridge Island, I fell into a revery about being 80 years old, with Ava in her early 50's as my meth-sex nurse, feeding me Viagra, then shooting me up, getting on top of me, and guiding my cock inside her.

When I pulled into the long, narrow forest trail leading to my driveway, I had no idea how I had gotten home safely.

* * *

Ava and I were sitting in the supercenter parking lot in Poulsbo, the only place in town with anything going on 24 hours a day. We would go there to get high when we had just scored drugs, and her kids were staying with her parents. I had just told her about the promise to my ex-wife to pay back the money she had lost on our failed real estate transaction during the Great Financial Crisis. Before I told Ava the exact monthly payment amount, she thought my intention was commendable.

"You're paying her how much? Did she own the house outright?" Ava's mouth was full of a drive-thru burger.

"No." I put my burger back into the paper bag because I'd lost my appetite.

"Then why would you agree to that?"

"I was a shitty husband. I put her through a lot of shit." I gazed out the window.

"That's too much. You could give me more if you didn't give her so much." Ava took another bite of her burger and shook her head.

Ava moved into my house not long after my ex-wife's brief visit. The wife of the guy who rented the spare bedroom to Ava got sick of her and her kids. Ava would tell me a couple of years later, after we had split and spent time separately on the streets, that the guy who moved her in had died. Before meeting Ava, I had once hired him to fell a tree on my property. When you're in drug circles, it's a frequent occurrence to hear that someone has suddenly died. These days, when scrolling through Facebook, the algorithm sometimes serves up his profile in the People You May Know feed. I hope someone considers claiming his profile to let him rest in peace.

When Ava and I would make up after a fight with quiet talk, she would recount the fork-in-the-road choice between moving in with me and an older client who offered to buy her a motorhome. She chose me because her boys liked me, and I was better-looking than the other guy. That part always sweetened me up.

Ava and I made the deal that would govern our living arrangements on the second night we spent together. She had nowhere to go, so she texted me to ask if I could get her a room to do her business that night. Wanting desperately to impress, I arranged a room at a casino. I met up with her and her cronies, but every time I moved to leave so she could receive clients, she suggested I stay.

"You could stay at my place. You don't have to pay rent. I'll give you enough to take care of you and the boys. You just gotta let me fuck you." Those were the terms I devised halfway through the night.

"That could work." Ava held my gaze.

That's how it was supposed to work. And it did, for a little while. We—she, her two boys, and I—were a little happy family. The boys were from two different fathers, both natives, so that you could mistake them for our kids. We made sure to clean up after ourselves and each other when it came to preparing and taking our drugs—I would keep a lookout for leftover syringes within a child's reach. She would sometimes clean up tiny meth shards that I might have spilled on the floor of the upstairs bedroom where we did our drugs together.

Ava talked me into letting her shoot me up with heroin, as that was her drug of choice, and we both wanted to share the experience, which I interpreted as her desire to be close. The first time was at the nearby casino hotel, after she had put the boys to bed. The shot she made me was too strong. I regained consciousness in bed with her beside me, staring with a smile.

"What happened?" I had no recollection of the evening after she shot me up.

"What do you mean?"

"I don't remember anything. Have I been out cold?" I wanted to throw up, but I couldn't get out of bed.

"No, silly," she laughed softly. "We've been talking like this the whole time, but you were kinda out of it."

The second time Ava and I tried communing with her drug of choice, I had booked a hotel for her to receive clients, and we made plans to meet there after she had closed up for business. She was excited and wanted to shoot me up before she left the house, having concocted a much less potent potion than the first time. But the stuff she had scored must have come from a strong batch because I was even sicker this time. Ava had to call an ex-client, who was dating one of her female dealers, to drive her to the hotel. He kept hitting on her while I was stuck at the house, sick as a dog. Henceforth, I swore off opioids of any kind. Still, I appreciated the gesture both times.

The terms of our deal specified that she and her kids could live in my house rent-free, along with a stipend, in return for sex a couple of times per week. After a month or so, Ava told me about an old drug-buddy who had just been released from jail: Could he stay with us for a little while?

His name was Pablo, and his presence signified our eventual downfall. He slept in Ava's room downstairs with the kids. She stopped coming to see me in my room upstairs. I told myself it was nothing. Pablo stayed for about a week the first time. He would be in and out of jail, staying with us for a little while each time he got out. The same pattern occurred, with Ava growing distant when Pablo was around, becoming more attentive when he'd go back to jail for months.

Ava stopped going on business dates because she knew I didn't like it. I gave her more than enough money to take care of herself and the kids, plus I bought all the heroin she needed. But we barely had sex anymore, and I was starting to feel used. She told me that she didn't like to have sex much ever since she'd gotten raped. After hearing this news, I felt the universal guilt of all men, so I just waited for her to approach me for sex. It didn't happen.

* * *

People came and went. Part of the terms of our agreement was that Ava would run the house and generate extra income by recruiting her connections to stay there and pay in kind—drugs or odd jobs that the house always required. Ava also sold parts of the ounce of heroin that I'd buy for her every month. I instructed her to meet her drug customers away from the house, as we lived in a private and quiet forest community where any disruption to the norm was questioned. She didn't get it— the neighbors invariably called the cops whenever they saw a rundown jalopy driving through their posh unpaved trails, and every time one of her customers would get pulled over, that person would have a warrant out for their arrest. The neighbors felt justified.

Around Christmas time, two of her cronies staying in the upstairs room invited their dealer to sleep over. Ava confessed that she had a crush on the dealer.

"Why would you tell me that?"

"Because we agreed to be open."

I was furious. By then, I had taken to spending days away from the house, living in my car, getting high on my own. I made gas money by shoplifting and then returning the items for cash (anything below $20) or a gift card.

The night Ava confessed her crush, I left the house, went to a casino, and won $700. I had never won that much gambling. I used to spend nights in casino parking lots when I'd spend days away from the house, like I was touring homelessness. After experiencing the winning high, the gene that my mother bequeathed to me, which gave me the predisposition for a gambling addiction, was activated like a sleeper cell. Every time I went to a casino from then on, I expected to win, wanted to win, needed that winning high.

The next day, as I looked forward to continuing my homelessness tour, Ava called me: her crush had stolen away in the wee hours of the morning, taking the remainder of her heroin stash and all of the Christmas presents for the kids that she had wrapped and placed lovingly under the tree. I returned and noticed that my work laptop was missing from the desk in the living room as well. I remembered debating whether I should take it with me before storming out, but I didn't want to feel like I was being forced out of my own home with all my things in tow while Ava's little crush remained in my house.

Christmas was still a few days out, and I'd just gotten paid. I didn't want to be in the house even more now, so I assured Ava I'd replace the kids' gifts. I could taste the freedom of living in my car purely on my wits for the next few days. The first place I went was the casino, promptly emptying my bank account. Whether I started out winning or losing, I would eventually drain my bank account—if I were winning, I'd think I could win more; when losing, I'd need to make up for what I had lost.

Luckily, I had filled my gas tank before losing all my money (and when I say 'all,' I mean every last cent), so I drove around the Puget Sound. I had enough drugs on me to last a day or two, so rather than paying for a motel room, I spent the night at the Fife rest stop and waited for the gym in my office building to open. The itinerary of my homelessness tours always encompassed Tacoma, Auburn, and Bellevue—the two casino hotspots and my office building. Ironically, I'd spend more time in the office during these tours than when I was living the double life of running drugs and playing at domesticity in Bainbridge Island.

I would boost new clothes to wear to work, and since I looked like an upstanding member of the establishment, store security never suspected a thing. This particular high-end discount store is the easiest and best place to boost—they have the brand names a man of my supposed stature is supposed to wear, most of which don't have security tags, so I could easily slip into the dressing rooms and slip on what I wanted underneath my outfit. New clothes in tow, I would make a pit stop at the office gym, shower, and make myself presentable. Then I'd park my car in a discrete area in the parking garage, crush up a fat line of meth, snort it, and walk into the office like I was the most normal of normies.

During lunchtime, I would go to the nearby mall and boost to get an adrenaline high to augment my ascending high from the fat line I had done before leaving the parking garage. On this day, though, I hoped to replace the kids' stolen presents. What luck—the supercenter had Amazon Kindles on special in an easy-to-reach display on the store floor, rather than behind the counter. I boosted two for each kid.

Back at the high-end discount store, I picked out a beautiful duffel bag for Ava, which took extra maneuvering. I then drove back to the house. When I arrived, I discovered that she had installed a new guy, along with the remaining people.

"He's gay," Ava assured me, "He's what's-his-name's brother. He can cook, fix things, and he's good with the kids."

"Cool. So, let's go on a long overdue overnight date night in the city."

Ava was into it. I booked a hotel room around the Amazon neighborhood in downtown Seattle the week after Christmas. We paid the squatter crew in heroin and meth to look after the house while we were gone. Ava dropped the kids off at her parents' house.

At the hotel, I made my new proposal to Ava. "I've decided to cut the money I'm paying my ex-wife and give it to you. You've earned it."

Ava hugged me and planted a peck on my cheek.

"Pablo is getting out of jail in a few days. He can stay with us again. Right?" She released her hug.

We didn't have sex that night either. Maybe she was waiting to see the money in her hand,.

When we returned to the house, everything looked normal. But we discovered a few days later that all hell had broken loose. Mr. Handyman-Cook-Babysitter had gotten so high that he was knocking on all the neighbors' doors and telling them about his paranoid delusions. Customers had come around looking for drugs, and every one of them had been pulled over by the cops and detained because they all had warrants.

We had to get out of there.

Luckily, my annual bonus was scheduled to hit my bank account in two weeks. It was big enough to pay over a year's worth of mortgage arrears and fix up the place to turn it into the Airbnb that I had promised Ava she could operate (one of the many promises I used to ply Ava's acquiescence). Instead, I chose to burn through the entire bonus and my significant monthly income in two months on the run.

This is the point at which I mark the beginning of my homelessness. Living on the streets with no permanent shelter starts as a liminal existence during which tragedies befall most people, precipitating a descent that rapidly gains momentum. A grave illness that demands the majority of financial resources; getting laid off from a once well-paying job; a divorce that leaves the dependent party with little-to-no resources and opportunities to recover; and no family or community support to provide a safety net.

One could make the argument that everyone who ends up homeless from such tragedies somehow contributed to their descent. For me, that argument is crystal clear—I had the resources to feed and water my addiction, which drove my underperformance and unethical behavior at work, partly driven by my divorce years before on which I refused to close the door, which in turn gave me the excuse to estrange myself from my dysfunctional birth family. Even though I now know that I have a genetic predisposition to a clinical disorder with co-occurring emotional maladies that were at the root of my anti-social and self-destructive behavior, I alone did it all, or at the very least let it happen, to myself.

* * *

Ava, the kids, and I stayed mainly at a family of hotels—of which I had become a gold member through international business trips, so racking up more points could further support our run—around the same areas where I had only recently camped out in my car during my homelessness tours. When we wanted to focus on gambling, we'd stay at a casino hotels. When we wanted to feel like a family, we'd rent a large Airbnb. The amount of meth and heroin that I would purchase for us doubled. I never told Ava how much money we were going through; she never asked.

Our run would end in Wenatchee, but I had no idea this would happen when Ava suggested that we visit her extended family there.

My boss called to ask when I planned on returning to work. Before I decided to go on the run, my boss brought me into his office for a talk. He said I didn't seem to be all there at work, and he needed me ready and able to manage the project on which I had been leading the strategy and planning the year before. I had mastered the tactic of staying high and awake for three days solid to pull together documents and presentations nearing the deadline, and got away with it. Still, it was apparent to everyone that I'd burned out, so he suggested that I take two weeks off, paid and without having to use my vacation days, to get my head screwed on straight. When my boss reached out to me while we were in our Wenatchee hotel, I mustered the desperate courage to write an email, confessing that I had charged up a personal storm on my corporate charge card and added a proposal for a repayment plan.

My boss advised me to take a few more days before returning to the office and let him know beforehand when I planned on arriving. On the day of my office homecoming, Ava was having one of her fits in finding a vein to shoot up. Sometimes, I was forced to take the kids for a walk while she spent hours looking for a suitable vein, remixing a couple more shots because the ones she had been trying to shoot would get too much blood mixed into them to be any good. We got back to Bellevue a few hours later than scheduled.

I entered the meeting room where my boss told me to meet him—he was sitting with an HR representative, and she looked pissed. She demanded that I return my laptop, security badge, and corporate charge card on the spot. The HR representative then told me what I had done was tantamount to stealing—the charge cards are meant only for business purposes. She continued that the company wouldn't press charges, but that I was trespassed from the premises.

I returned to the car in the parking garage and told Ava the news.

"I knew it." She shook her head.

A couple of days later, Ava and the kids left to return to Wenatchee. She said she wanted to spend time with her extended family alone because she hadn't had a chance to bond with them well with me in tow. I guess I understood. Something didn't seem right—she was putting on her makeup while in the driver's seat of my car as I stood in a restaurant parking lot in SeaTac, as she reiterated that she wouldn't be away very long. I felt queasy as I walked to my hotel.

Ava didn't answer my texts all night. So, I found a girl online and hired her for a date. During major life events, I had this habit of seeing a prostitute just to talk. I wouldn't set things up that way upfront because I never planned on just talking. I'd pay upfront, but then I'd find myself desiring an empathetic ear more than anything. I could tell a prostitute things that only someone else with fucked-up lived experience could understand, such as how I'm a drug addict and prefer transactional relationships with prostitutes.

I did just that the night before I was scheduled to drive from Silicon Valley, where I had lived and worked for over two years, back to Los Angeles to live with my ex-wife and supposedly assume the mortgage on her house before the Financial Crisis hit. And I did this again with the call girl who visited me after Ava absconded with my car. I told my street-walking therapist how I'd transferred most of my final paycheck, which included two weeks' vacation pay, into Ava's PayPal account. I felt guilty about blowing my annual bonus and the last two months of paychecks, but now Ava had been ghosting me.

"Doesn't look good," my therapist observed.

I told her how I'd been fired and was thinking about investing the remaining money in drugs to sell full-time.

"Maybe you should think about going into financial scams. I bet you'd be good at it," she advised.

The next day, Ava finally responded to my texts, but they were short and cryptic. Then, a week later, Ava spilled the beans—she had been galivanting around with Pablo, whom she picked up in Suquamish after dropping me off in SeaTac. They'd blown all the money in her PayPal account, getting high and fucking, her revenge for my broken promises that ruined her dreams of managing the house as an Airbnb while her kids attended the highly regarded Bainbridge Island schools.

"Why Pablo? He's so ugly."

"Jealous much?"

Ava returned my car the day after her vengeful confession. She hadn't been setting me up. Instead, the vision of a stable and well-to-do lifestyle so tantalizingly within her grasp was the collateral damage of the untenable lifestyle I had been hell-bent on destroying and in which I had brilliantly succeeded.

Chapter 4

Professional Drug Addict

Not only did I think that I was I special, but I also thought I was singular, entitled to receive the gifts of the universe without having to try or work.

I would discover in recovery that all addicts think of themselves as special. Mainly, this feeling of superiority is overcompensation for the intractable self-perception of abject unworthiness, like a beauty filter for social media selfies.

Our ancient forebears designed cultural initiations from adolescence to adulthood to be arduous in order to teach children to not only trust but also revere the process. The myth of the gatekeeper guarding the entrance to a cave or castle containing spiritual gold is the essence of the necessity of paying archetypal dues.

But I wanted nothing to do with waiting. I wanted it all now.

The height of my hubris was equal to the depth of my self-pity.

Taking advantage of a good shortcut requires flexible ethics. Different from efficiency, which is morally ambivalent and can be used for good or evil. A quantum leap, on the other hand, requires sophisticated criminality. That's where Aiden came in.

Right after I got my car back from Ava, I skipped the ferry and drove from Poulsbo to the Airbnb where Aiden had set up headquarters in Ravenna.

Aiden was in a different abode every couple of weeks—he had a collection of buttoned-up hangers-on who acted as credible fronts for him, booking posh hotels and Airbnbs in their names so that Aiden could remain undercover. His upstanding cadre adored him and were enamored by the insider access to his sordid and exhilarating underworld while appreciating the safe distance their clean contributions granted them. I was no different. But now, newly unemployed, single, and entirely out of cash, my intention was a down-and-dirty career change.

I needed money to buy enough meth to keep myself sufficiently high, while selling the remainder at a profit to live on and buy more. That's the formula. So, I called my father. Although I had been estranged from my family pretty much from the time I had moved to Scotland almost 20 years since this very phone call—visiting every once in a while, but never living close enough to be fully integrated, and then becoming entirely estranged since my relocation from California back to the Seattle area—my father made the effort to keep in touch with me. It was his way of keeping me in the fold. With this phone call, I planned on abusing his good intentions.

I told him that I had been laid off. If this excuse worked at every job interview during my tech career, after getting fired from a previous job for the underperformance in the second year of every job following the preordained overachieving of the first year on the job, with both levels of performance fueled by overuse of and inevitable crash from cocaine, then it should work with my father. I then told him that I was launching a startup with my new business partner, Aiden (that wasn't a lie—at the very least, it was my intention), and I was going to use my severance package (lie—Ava had spent the lion's share on her escapade with Pablo) to fund the business. However, we needed about $1500 to pay for LLC incorporation fees (total lie) and wanted to reserve the severance package proceeds for business operations.

"So, what's this business?"

"Import-export. My business partner has connections in Latin America for goods with a good-sized demand but difficult to find." There was a pause, so I quickly filled it, "If you want to know the truth, my business partner is in the Italian mafia and wants to start a legitimate business. I lend him legitimacy."

I had taken a calculated risk—growing up, it seemed to me that my father had a fascination with criminality, though he never committed to it like I did—my father had rich, ambiguous associates with whom he had done business, but ultimately cut off relations when he remembered his integrity.

"Italian mafia." He chuckled softly. "OK, I'll send you the money. Good luck."

I went up to the small but stylish Airbnb apartment that one of Aiden's fronts rented for him. The woman who, later that night, would protest that she could never take money in exchange for sex, was lounging lazily on the sofa when I entered. She started loading a bong with a decent shard of meth, instantly curing her laziness. Aiden and I had been messaging each other more than usual over the past few days, which meant a furious pace, so he already knew everything that had happened with Ava and the plans I'd been hatching.

"Got the money," I proclaimed.

"Every professional I know who's tried selling drugs as a full-time job has ended up in prison."

"I'm different, though." I walked out to the balcony and lit a cigarette.

"No, you're not."

"What else am I supposed to do?" Then I remembered the assessment from my recent session with a prostitute-counselor. "Financial scams?"

"Now you're talking." Aiden handed me an ounce of meth. "You can write my biography, too."

I met Aiden through Tess, his consigliere at the time. I met her on MeetMe, my prevailing platform for new drug sources and women who acted like prostitutes but wanted mainly to hang out with a guy who could supply drugs in exchange for sitting around and looking pretty with the promise (but not the guarantee) of sex. Tess's job was to attract new business and screen them. I would discover later, when Aiden abruptly dropped Tess after a year-long partnership because of some vague violation of trust that she had committed, that Aiden's methodology entailed love-bombing whomever he had chosen to be his eventual right-hand, lavishing them with attention and gifts to influence and manipulate.

Aiden was the one who used this term when I once made the observation that he had a gift for quickly, almost immediately, gaining the trust and adulation of new people whom he had chosen. Love-bombing's goal of influence and exploit is the source of its violent essence, as this strategy is considered abuse in and of itself, leading to further abuse, both psychological and physical.

Aiden would always pad the ounces of heroin and meth that he sold me. Both products were of the utmost quality, uncut by fillers while under his care, thus retaining their purity. Ava was always impressed by the healthy portions and strength of the stuff I'd bring home. Aiden's generosity allowed me to be a good provider.

Aiden wanted professional drug addicts around him. I sealed the deal with Tess and Aiden by sending my LinkedIn profile. Through Tess, Aiden sealed the deal with me by reciprocating with his LinkedIn profile—he presented himself as a serial entrepreneur, with a headshot of a young professional who looked like he could have been the captain of his high school soccer team. I imagined him sauntering the school halls wearing a letterman's jacket while selling cocaine to the teachers on the down low. I had spent two decades nurturing my business profile, but this guy beat my number of followers fivefold. Aiden's gate to the underground was an order of magnitude higher caliber than the entrance where I met Kaylee.

On the fateful day of our first meeting, I was summoned to the middle-class neighborhood of Wallingford, where Tess had rented an Airbnb apartment under her name for Aiden to use as his lair. Tess opened the door and informed me that Aiden was out making deliveries to the ring of erotic espresso stands in which he had partial ownership.

A few minutes later, Aiden walked in. He shook my hand and took off his jacket to reveal the pistol holster around his shoulder—he kept it on throughout our initial meeting. After some pleasantries, Aiden unveiled a massive bong, went to the freezer to get ice cubes, which he placed in the water chamber, and retrieved a substantial bag brimming with meth. Aiden offered the bong to me first. I had been at my office that morning, preparing for a big meeting in which vice presidents and other corporate luminaries would be in attendance, and the extended break to make this surreptitious rendezvous had made me antsy.

"I have to get back to the office after this for a big meeting, so I don't want to get too high."

"You have to get high with us. I wanna know you're legit." Aiden stared at me.

"If you insist."

After passing the test, Aiden instructed me to go through Tess for all future business transactions.

I contacted Tess the next time I needed product. But the time after that, she didn't respond soon enough (i.e., immediately). As I didn't have Aiden's number, I decided to contact him on LinkedIn.

ME: "Hey- haven't heard from Tess and really need to do some business tonight. Don't have your number, so I hope you don't mind me reaching out. Reach me at xxx-xxx-xxxx. Thanks."

I didn't hear from Aiden that night, so I had to go through a different source. Five days later, Aiden messaged me back.

AIDEN: "Hey- I just saw this. Call me via Signal at xxx-xxx-xxx or check your Snapchat if you do not have Signal."

Signal is the most secure messaging app in the world, and Snapchat, at the time, offered privacy features that Facebook and regular texting didn't offer to the discerning underworld businessman and his flock. From then on, we communicated exclusively through Signal.

It didn't take long for an opportunity to arise that I seized to develop a trustworthy partnership with Aiden. About a week later, he called asking if I could rent a car for him—the guy who usually did it for him every two weeks needed to lay low for a while.

"I don't have a credit card right now. My credit sucks."

"I need to make my deliveries tonight, and now I'm stuck."

"I'll be your driver." I didn't think twice and drove to Aiden's Airbnb in record time.

"You like molly?" When I arrived, Aiden was organizing and packing his products. He pulled a large capsule from his considerable stash and showed it to me.

"MDMA? Love it. Well, I loved ecstasy but haven't seen it in decades?"

"I cooked it. Molly is one atom away from meth, so I always make some when I make my own meth."

"I never knew that." I was amazed. "Not sure if it's a good idea since I'm driving."

"So, there's a few things I should tell you. We're going to meet up with some cartel folks. They might get a little spooked since they've never seen you before. They might kidnap you." Aiden handed me the capsule.

"I think I'll take that molly. If I get kidnapped, I'll feel so good that I won't be stressed." At once, I was thrilled and scared shitless.

Taking the capsule turned out to be a bad idea—it was so strong when it hit, my eyes were rolling, and all I could see were tracers.

Aiden was forced into the driver's role.

"I thought you were a professional."

I sat in the passenger seat, slumped over. I felt sick whenever I raised my head.

"I am a professional. But that stuff you mixed is too strong."

"You're saying I should use less? Hmm. If it's that strong, I can still charge the same and increase my profit margin. Thanks for being my guinea pig." Aiden smiled.

"Glad I could be of service, since I was supposed to be your driver."

Being in one vulnerable situation after another while driving with someone all night is a forced bonding experience similar to the brothers-in-arms effect. Aiden met with his cartel distributors, and they talked for a while. When he returned to the car, he informed me that they had decided against kidnapping me. I was relieved.

As Aiden drove and I slumped, he imparted a litany of incriminating knowledge about the mafia business: He had complete immunity around Seattle, which had cost his organization $100K (like buying a luxury car off a dealership lot)—didn't always work, though, as all it took was one cop with integrity to pull him over and search his car, so we were mostly free to do whatever we wanted; still, there would always be a slight chance of ending up in jail until one of the mafia-purchased cops cleaned up the righteous mess of a clean cop; the guy who usually rented cars for him was a DEA agent the organization had in their pocket, but he was getting paranoid and needed a break; Aiden was a "seen man," meaning he was officially known to the organization but could never be formally inducted as a "made man" because he wasn't of full Italian heritage, though he received the full rights and protections of a "made man" since he contributed directly to the organization's business activities.

People with significant secret lives can seem illogically transparent about details that the mainstream would expect them to keep close. But there's an unexpected twist to this behavior: if you don't believe their incredible tales, then you won't take them seriously, and the only time you might divulge their secrets is to ridicule them; if you do believe their accounts, then you treat the information with reverence. Either way, their secrets are safe.

Aiden's last stop for the night was a motel in Kent. In the room, a large woman held court like a ghetto queen, with her courtiers scattered throughout, all of whom were wasted out of their minds. The Queen of Kent caringly scooted over to make room on the bed for Aiden. One of her courtiers stood up from his armchair and motioned for me to take it. I gladly wilted into it.

"Who's the lightweight?" The Queen of Kent finished surveying the freshly delivered products and lifted her suspicious gaze towards me.

* * *

Aiden developed his business acumen while selling drugs as a youth for a Seattle street gang. He claimed to have had a typical middle-class upbringing. He didn't elaborate, as if keeping information that might contradict his claim, but the way he spoke was proper. In middle school, he joined a faction of the Crips. Since he was short and skinny, he leveraged his tenacious nature and turned it into a fearless attitude, a vehicle he rode to the top of the leaderboard in terms of marijuana and crack cocaine sales.

Despite becoming a big deal on his streets, witnessing his gang folks get murdered or sent to prison made the whole endeavor untenable. So, at the age when he should have been in high school, Aiden met members of a Christian youth ministry, who offered him a way out. They helped steer him to bible college, where he received a degree in theology, honing the skills of a preacher that could summon people to join his flock. He also learned information technology and landed a job with Microsoft after college.

In the mid-2000s, Aiden parlayed this experience and the business acumen he absorbed on the streets to fashion himself into a tech entrepreneur, launching a software company in Atlanta. He quickly sold his startup and was looking for a new challenge. That's when the mafia called, enticing him back to Seattle to spearhead new business activities.

Aiden's 40th birthday was fast approaching, and he wanted to retire from the game. His thinking behind the desire to publish his biography stemmed from the grim statistics of the life expectancy of drug dealers—he should have been dead by now. But no one just leaves the organization—it's a lifetime commitment. So, he hatched a plan to publish a tell-all, naming names. If anyone from the organization even thought about coming after him to ensure his silence, the existence of his biography would make them think twice, as any of the named names would immediately become suspects. Equally, the propagation of a tell-all would render the very reason behind his assassination a moot point, as nothing could silence the ongoing presence of a published book. At least, that was his theory.

The thought of being Aiden's ghostwriter invoked a guttural fear I had never felt before. The adrenaline was intoxicating. I wanted to do it.

But neither of us followed up. We were more enamored with the idea than the reality. However, the fear that his biography might exist turned the night of his 40th birthday into a quest.

About a week before Aiden's birthday, he intimated his intention of getting all his associates together for a strategy offsite—the first convening of every one of his hand-picked people outside of the organization. He wanted to do it on his birthday as both a symbolic launch of his next phase and a literal launch of his new endeavor. But then, on the scheduled day, I received cryptic, nonsensical messages from him. I was also running out of drugs, so I needed to meet with him.

ME: "What's up? When and where are all of us going to meet?"

AIDEN: "I have to reschedule."

ME: "Ok, but I still NEED to meet."

AIDEN: "Bring the original manuscript of the book with you."

ME: "What are you talking about?"

AIDEN: "I need the book. All the copies you have."

ME: "You know there's no book yet."

AIDEN: "You heard me. I need all the copies."

I knew this was not Aiden. Not only had we never worked on the project earnestly, but a tech guy would never have asked for all the copies of a manuscript that would have lived exclusively on my laptop.

Whoever this person was on the other end had done something with and to Aiden. I started receiving messages from some of Aiden's other cronies. They had also been contacted by the kidnapper, trying to get bits of information on Aiden's retirement plans. For the rest of the night, I was switching back and forth between messaging Aiden's kidnapper to get information on his whereabouts and coordinating with the cronies. The kidnapper sent us on a wild goose chase, dropping obscure clues about their location at the time and where they might be headed.

The kidnapper continued interrogating me about the book. No matter my protestations of its existence, the kidnapper wouldn't believe me. Finally, at dawn, the kidnapper decided to lead me to Aiden—the big rental SUV he had been driving for weeks was parked at an industrial dock near the east side of the West Seattle Bridge. Aiden would later comment that there were a lot of dead bodies buried under that dock's cement. When I found him, he was out cold, his hands and feet tied up. He startled when I woke him. I left my car there and drove Aiden back in his SUV to his current Airbnb near Highway 99, about a mile off Aurora Avenue.

Aiden went straight to bed, helped by his current GFE from an ever-revolving cast. After a couple of minutes, he asked her to summon me.

"I need a tarp, some rope, and a gun," Aiden barked, and then immediately fell back asleep.

I was flat broke, so I asked his current GFE if she knew where he kept his money. She looked at me, followed by a pause brimming with doubt.

"You heard him. Right? I need about $300 to get all that." I didn't blink.

She finally relented, opening the nightstand drawer, peeling off three bills, and handing them to me.

I spent the day driving around, gathering the items with obscure meanings, but the meaning behind the gun was obvious. As I was crossing the Tacoma Narrows Bridge and entering the Peninsula to hook up with some folks who could get a gun, I got a call from Aiden.

"I need you to return with the money."

"Ok. But I still need to pick up that last thing you asked for."

"I need you to come back now." Aiden's tone had become polite.

I complied and headed back to the Airbnb.

"I needed money for gas, and I was hungry." I gave Aiden the tarp, rope, and the $175 I didn't spend on a gun.

"What was the last thing?" Aiden surveyed the items with a smirk.

"A gun."

"Ha. Those are the items my godmother would use in an assassination."

The following day, Aiden called the various customers to whom he had scheduled deliveries on his birthday night, asking whether he had arrived and, if so, whether anyone accompanied him. They all said he was with a woman, but Aiden knew he hadn't started the night with a woman, though whether he had company at any point was still fuzzy. His customers all described the woman as quiet and tall. Then, one of his customers made an observation that clicked—this woman had abnormally big hands.

It all came back to Aiden: he had started the night with his security detail, a soft-spoken, unassuming, government-trained killing machine, the Seattle mafia version of Leon in the movie The Professional. Aiden always wondered whether his security detail had a thing for him. Turns out he did, and he acted on it on Aiden's birthday—he had roofied Aiden with a date-rape drug, dressed up as a woman, accompanied him on his rounds…and who knows what else.

A few days later, I called Aiden and asked what the organization had discovered about Seattle Leon.

"He's been taken care of."

"He kept demanding that I give him all the manuscript copies of your biography. How did he know about it?"

"I told him. But he knew that we hadn't done any real work on it. Hmm. Just the thought of it must have scared some people." Aiden looked away.

I felt uncomfortable at the Airbnb, which is ironic, seeing as I had rescued Aiden...well, at least I was the one who found and brought him back to safety. For as long as Aiden and I had run together, I never stayed over at his camps—if I spent the night, it was because we had stayed up all night partying and strategizing. But the night I returned with the tarp, rope, and leftover money, there was a weird vibe. I put it down to the strangeness of the events and Aiden needing to recover.

Rather than returning to my usual transitional lifestyle of staying in my car and hitting up casinos, I left Aiden's camp and returned to the Bainbridge house. I found it in shambles—the place had been ransacked, and someone dared to steal the old, heavy woodstove. I tried to chill for a bit on the refurbished Chinese opium bed that weighed as much as two dead bodies, but then I heard the minuscule tip-tapping of multiple tiny claws in the attic—the rodents had reclaimed the abandoned property. I got the hell out of there. As I drove out of the polite forest community, I noticed a police car parked on the side of the road. I vowed to myself that I would never return.

Luckily, Aiden had messaged, saying he had moved camp to the Queen of Kent's motel, along with his room number.

When I arrived, I was met by a guy who told me that Aiden wasn't there and that I could wait in his room. So, I followed him in, whereupon he slammed me down onto one of the beds.

"So, you're the motherfuckin' mole." The henchman had his hands around my throat.

Before I could say anything, the door opened and in came the Queen of Kent. She demanded that I give her my phone so she could search it. I unlocked my phone with the most stone-cold expression I could summon. She snatched the phone and scrolled through my messages, trying to find incriminating evidence that I was in on Aiden's kidnapping. This charade perturbed more than scared me. My interrogators weren't very good at their jobs. There were bags of leftover fast food next to the television on the dresser, and as I hadn't eaten, I started snacking on them.

After a few insufferable minutes of this shit show, Aiden walked in, wearing an expression of seemingly feigned surprised.

"What's going on in here?"

"We thought he was the mole, but he's clean." The Queen of Kent was not pleased.

"I didn't ask you to do this," Aiden scolded.

"I made an executive decision," the Queen of Kent beamed.

"You guys can go." Aiden opened the door, holding it as the Queen of Kent and her henchman filed out.

As my interrogators left, I followed them to the walkway and lit a cigarette. The henchman approached me to shake my hand. I accepted it.

"Sorry about that, man. We're just trying to look out for our man Aiden." I nodded my head.

Halfway through my cigarette, Aiden came out and stood next to me. After a pause, he apologized for them in his way.

"I didn't ask them to do that. But is there something else you haven't told me?" Aiden's tone held an undercurrent of pride.

"I didn't have anything to do with your kidnapping."

"I know you. That's not what I meant. Have you been through something like this before? I mean, you have a stutter sometimes, and when I walked in, you were all calm and cool. You sat there eating their lunch. You weren't even fazed."

"Look, I've never been in this life before. That's the first time I've been interrogated as a potential mole," I looked at him incredulously, then it all came to me. "In my corporate job, I have to get up in front of high-powered executives, pitching for company resources and money for my projects. I have to stand there, alone, while they eviscerate my presentation. What they're really doing is cutting me to shreds. Then, I have to go back to the drawing board and patch up the holes in my pitch. After that, I have to get back up there, alone, and defend my livelihood until I get it right. I swim with sharks. Your little people are tadpoles."

Aiden smiled and patted me on the back.

Later that night, the henchman and his girl approached me, asking if they could borrow my car. I felt so vindicated that I didn't think twice about giving him my keys. Equally, I thought the gesture would sway him into my court. I never saw my car again.

I told Aiden what had happened. He just shook his head in disbelief, wondering why I had fallen, again, for a beginner's street ploy.

"You might swim with sharks, but you're still a mark, my boy." Aiden put his hand on my shoulder and squeezed...hard.

To make myself feel better, I reminded myself that I had stopped making payments on the car months ago, so I figured the repo men would eventually track the henchman down.

* * *

"I'm sorry, Mr. Leyva, but the credit card your secretary sent along has been declined," the hotel receptionist informed me.

"Hmm. That's odd. Would you mind if I sit in the lobby while I contact her to see what's the matter?"

"Sure. Just let me know," the receptionist agreed politely.

I texted Tilly.

ME: "It's not working."

TILLY: "You're not acting right."

ME: "Don't patronize me. I know how to act in these situations. I've traveled for business around the world. I need new numbers."

TILLY: "Ok, give me a min."

I opened my laptop, recently purchased on Amazon, so that I looked the part.

Half an hour later, the receptionist called me up. "You're all set, Mr. Leyva," she said while handing me the key card to the room.

I thanked the receptionist, then texted Aiden and Tilly the room number.

The day after the amateur interrogation, Aiden showed me a slip of paper with a written list of three number sequences. I recognized immediately that they were credit card numbers. He purchased them from Tilly, a woman on the Queen of Kent's court. Some of the most intelligent people I have ever met were on the streets. Tilly was summa cum laude amongst her peers. When I once commented that she had a world-class mind, she looked at me curiously, ready to defend herself.

"What do you mean?"

"You could've been accepted into MIT." I didn't add 'if her circumstances had been different,' but that part was on my mind.

Tilly was a master at generating numbers, a scam that entails finding a recent credit card and leveraging the Luhn algorithm, which the credit industry uses to produce the number sequence on credit and debit cards, to generate new sequences that fit the industry-wide algorithm.

A small percentage of these newly generated sequences will have active credit limits. The active numbers are a mixture of credit cards that have yet to be issued and ones currently in the possession of their rightful owners. To identify which numbers were, in fact, active, you need the merchant manual authorization phone number of a large banking institution, along with a genuine merchant number. The process entails calling that phone number, entering your merchant number, manually charging a small amount, and then seeing what happens. This is the same process that gas stations and restaurants use to preauthorize credit cards.

When Tilly taught me the ropes, I started to thirst for the tone of the automated voice that proclaimed, "Approved"—it got me so high. Contrarily, there is a distinctly underwhelming, even somber, tone to the automated voice stating, "Declined."

I was enamored with the romantic notion of finding live but unissued number sequences. I was Robin Hood, taking from the big bad credit system and giving to the poor and disenfranchised. I put the thought of accidentally happening upon someone's actual credit card number out of my head.

The drawback of generating new number sequences was that the process did not create the CVV—card verification value, also known as CSC (card security code) and CID (card identification number). Finding this information feels like hitting the Powerball or Mega Millions lottery, but only financial insiders can get it. To cash out, or derive some value from, a generated number, you must use it in places and platforms that don't require the CVV. To this day, a handful of e-commerce platforms do not require CVVs. As a product manager for tech companies, one of my responsibilities was anticipating and managing fraud levels: Fraud is expected in every enterprise, so managing the amount at defined acceptable levels is standard practice; this knowledge led me to surmise that large e-commerce platforms make more money with lower fraud protections, as the credit system ultimately pays a sizable number of such transactions.

The other lucrative method to derive value from generated numbers for the liminally housed is booking hotels, which entails a social engineering element: Hotels allow a person to book rooms for a group using a paper form in which the credit card information is written—it's called a hotel credit card authorization form and does not require the CVV; this method is generally used by administrative assistants booking multiple rooms for a team of employees, but it can also be used by the person responsible for organizing an event for a familiar group of people; the booking form, along with a (fake) copy of the credit card and the responsible person's (fake) ID, is then faxed to hotel management; all the person, or people, checking into the hotel need to show is their driver license.

Since I was the only one in Aiden's crew who hadn't yet lost their ID, and as I was an expert at staying in nice hotels, that role fell to me. I reveled in it.

When Aiden arrived at the hotel, Tilly was still on her way, so I wanted to show him my new find before she arrived, a website on the gray internet, not quite the full-fledged dark internet because the listing showed up on a Google search for "generated numbers." The homepage displayed a graphic of the Guy Fawkes mask used by Anonymous, the tech (anti-)terrorist collective. The site offered an automated numbers generator, which required the first 12 digits of a credit card, from which it would spit out 10,000 new combinations, as well as a feature that automatically tested whether a specific number sequence had an active credit limit.

Aiden had a broad smile on his face. Then he got serious, "Don't show Tilly."

I didn't say anything. I may not have had any ethics, but I subscribed to the code of Honor Amongst Thieves. Tilly had shown me the ropes of this particular sector of the underworld. It didn't feel right keeping this information from her. I sensed that Aiden's intent wasn't merely to keep this resource for ourselves. It was a test of my loyalty.

As much as I had submitted to the codependent's compliance patterns in our partnership—extreme loyalty, remaining in harmful situations too long, compromising my values and integrity to avoid rejection or anger, putting aside my interests to do what he wanted, hypervigilant regarding his feelings, refraining from expressing my opinions when they differed from his, and making decisions without regard to the consequences—I couldn't bring myself to give up the only code to which I subscribed that even resembled ethics and fair play. Also, I was getting tired of being his consiglieri—it wasn't paying off.

When Tilly finally showed up to the room, I opened my laptop to show her my new find…in front of Aiden so that I couldn't be accused of going behind his back.

"Yeah, I know that site. The Feds are onto it, so the automatic tester doesn't work. But the numbers it generates are still good."

After two days in that room, the hotel management stopped accepting faxed credit card numbers—they demanded a physical credit card. Aiden went his separate way, and I left with Tilly's crew. We were all supposed to meet up the next day, but I didn't hear from Aiden, so I just let it be.

And that was the end of our running partnership.

Over the next few months, I would see Aiden two more times.

Once, when I successfully scammed my own profile to book a handful of rooms with Tilly and her crew, she invited Aiden to stay with us. He mostly stayed away from me, so I obliged.

Lastly, a few months later, after I had burned through my credibility with the hotels and motels around Highway 99, I heard that Aiden was shacking up in an apartment in Lynnwood with a young couple he had adopted as his new apprentice gangsters. I found myself in Lynwood and had no place to stay, so I hit him up, offering active generated numbers and a scheme I had hatched to use them to create counterfeit credit card checks. All I needed was someone like him to help me forge the checks, provide profiles to associate with the generated numbers, and a fresh-faced accomplice to cash them. He and his new crew could offer me exactly what I needed. We both thought this scenario was serendipity.

Aiden claimed that he had given up the dealer game and was making money solely on buying profiles on the dark web. I would use the direct merchant card servicing phone number and new merchant codes that I had gathered to check whether the profiles he had purchased were any good. It was almost like old times, but this scenario didn't last a week—the money we generated wasn't enough. His desperation must have been building before my arrival, as it reached a crescendo one day when he decided to dip his toe back into his old scene and make some quick cash selling dope.

"One more time to tide is over."

While he was out, he sent me a text asking for help—his rental car had been automatically shut down—it was a carshare and worked on an hourly basis. The dark-web credit card he had associated with it had been abruptly declined.

ME: "I wish I could help, but I don't have the CVVs for my generated numbers."

AIDEN: "I'm out here putting my ass on the line, and you can't come through. What good are you?"

ME: "I'm sorry."

AIDEN: "You've gone downhill since I knew you. And all you did while you were there was sit around and go outside every hour to smoke. I want you gone."

ME: "I left a duffel bag in your trunk with some nice stuff that I boosted. They should fit you. Keep it."

AIDEN: "Whatever."

ME: "I'm still going to write your story."

AIDEN: "Sure, pal."

Aiden had spent an inordinate amount of energy making me feel irreplaceable and idealized so I'd stick around. I did the same for him. We put each other on pedestals, guaranteeing a precipitous and final fall. The inescapable devaluations that we executed on each other—that I had devolved into a homeless guy hustling on the streets with pieces of paper in my pocket that held nothing but promises, and he aged poorly as a battle-worn mafioso who couldn't make a career change stick while hourly rental cars shut down on him—had reached their nadir.

I clung to the notion that I could someday regain my value and enshrine his memory in a fitting tale. I will never write the biography that Aiden wanted. What we have is this chapter.

Chapter 5

Grand Identity Theft Auto

As an impressionable English major in college, I read about the upwardly transient creatives residing in Parisian hotels in the early 20th century and found the lifestyle irresistibly romantic.

I wanted to be like The Moderns—F. Scott Fitzgerald, T.S. Eliot, and Ernest Hemingway—living in Paris in the 1920s when the City of Light was as cheap to live in as Seattle in the late 1990s. During both eras, young people worldwide seeking urban adventure and professional opportunities flocked to affordable cultural meccas. Okay, so Seattle isn't anywhere close to Paris in historical esteem, but the Grunge and tech scenes made the Northwest outpost an attractive destination for Gen X-ers and Millennials before Microsoft became part of the establishment and Amazon blew up.

The angst-ridden Moderns were the disillusioned generation of their time, writing about the alienation of modern life during rampant postwar industrialization. As for me, I was so disillusioned with my own modern tech double life that I deliberately blew it up, eventually finding myself on the streets with nothing but underhanded knowledge that promised to let me leverage the expertise I had gained in the establishment to scam the system. I envisioned living in hotels for the rest of my life like a modern-day Modern with a bougie backpack. However, the reality would be that I would turn to this illusion whenever I needed to disassociate from the squalor of dingy motel rooms, bus stops, and homeless encampments.

My running partnership with Tilly was short-lived. That's the main characteristic of the vast majority of partnerships and relationships on the streets—meet in a seemingly serendipitous occasion, create an instant bond predicated on some common interest that revolved around drug-seeking, run together for as long as both parties found each other useful, and then disband just as quickly, usually when a shinier fleeting interest catches one partner's fancy, or the other partner becomes estranged through justice-system involvement.

The drawback of shacking up in fancy hotels using generated numbers is that its very nature doesn't lend itself to the strategic time required to set up the next stay. Perpetrators of this corner of the underworld always try to push the limits of the validity of the generated numbers. After a couple of days, the generated number gets shut down. Then, hotel management inevitably gets suspicious—that's when they typically stop accepting any further hotel credit card authorization forms. Without a valid credit card, they'll kick you out. Sometimes, this happens even before the generated numbers get shut down. All it takes is a crusading night manager who's been scammed one too many times—night managers have carte blanche to kick anyone out based on mere suspicion, which is precisely what happened during the penultimate time I saw Aiden.

Tilly had run out of generated numbers that worked (or so she claimed), so we spent most of the day waiting at the hotel entrance with no strategy for the next stay. Finally, I looked at my favorite hotel app, unsure of what else to do and hoping to find something I might have overlooked. The recent fraudulent hotel stays had accumulated enough points for a free night. I told the others I'd book a room at my favorite four-star hotel on the Highway, and then text the room number after checking in.

The hotel is a sprawling campus with a several-story building at the center and seven interconnected wings. The main hotel entrance opens to a cozy living room-style area replete with a large fireplace ornamented in the only 1970s-era stonework that has aged well—thin, elongated, rough-hewn stones. Although the property has become slightly frayed at the edges, it retains a cool vintage glamor. Every room has a balcony, which delights smokers. I saw it as the perfect blend of glamour and street cred for the contemporary Modern.

I texted the room number to Tilly, and a cavalcade of her extended crew arrived, left, and replaced each other throughout the night. They all spent the night hanging out, taking drugs, and getting to know me. A couple of the guys were my age, having made a career of identity theft—riding high one minute and blowing it all the next, because that's how every hustler handles easy money. However, obtaining so-called easy money requires the same, if not more, time and effort than any legitimate means.

The next day, we sat around the lobby fireplace with nowhere to go... again. I checked out a different hotel app and noticed I had enough points to get a free night for a much less glamorous hotel a few blocks down the Highway. I booked a room and headed down the road, but when I tried to check in, the receptionist asked for a credit card deposit. My favorite highway hotel didn't ask for one because I had reached the highly trusted gold level. But this less desirable hotel chain didn't have such a built-in loyalty deference.

When I returned to the lobby with my tail between my legs, one of the career ID thieves immediately laid into me with the admonition that, if I was going to make it in this game, I needed to be ultra detail-oriented. I sized him up, surveyed the rest of the rag-tag crew, and realized that they were beneath me. Likewise, Tilly wasn't good-looking enough to offset this feeling. Without saying another word, I turned around and walked out the lobby doors. Never saw any of them again on the streets.

Up to that point, I had exhibited my default porous boundaries with Tilly and her crew—difficulty saying no to others' requests or demands, accepting abuse or neglect, highly dependent on other people and their opinions, and fear of rejection. Since I never learned how to set boundaries, I would become angry and reactionary when boundary setting was necessary, often going to the other extreme of rigid boundaries—

unwilling to compromise and quick to cut people off without any prospect of a second chance.

* * *

THEFT IN THE THIRD DEGREE | MISDEMEANOR | SEATAC MUNICIPAL COURT

I usually needed a few days to contrive a hotel stay, so some nights I was left to alternate devices, which typically meant hanging around the airport, the only all-night public facility in the area, and one with which I was familiar and comfortable navigating as though I belonged. After such nights, I would usually head to one of the three-star hotels within walking distance to grab a free coffee. Sometimes, if I had recently boosted a new outfit and a brand-name backpack preferred by the business-hipster traveler, allowing me to look exceptionally stylish, I would venture into a hotel that served complimentary breakfast to its guests.

On the day I would be jailed for the first time, I was having coffee in the lobby of yet another hotel on the Highway, trying to pass for a casual tech guy on the last day of his business trip. The guy sitting next to me was on his phone, discussing the need to find another hotel. He appeared like a business-hipster traveler with a snowboarder ethos. My gut told me it was all a ruse. I needed a new accomplice and figured that if this guy could pull off looking the part at a three-star hotel, he might make a useful running mate. I decided to interview him.

"I can get a room at any hotel. Have you heard of generated numbers?"

"I can generate them manually."

"Damn, bro. I need an online generator." I was impressed, so I had a little trouble keeping my voice down.

We both got up to refill our coffee cups. When we returned to our armchairs, he told me his condensed story: He didn't have much schooling, but he had always had a facility for math; he grew up in Texas and got a job as the personal assistant to one of the richest men in the area; he was living what he considered the high life at the time, but then, he got into some serious trouble and had to leave state, leaving behind his daughter and baby-mama; he'd been on the run for about 10 years, using his knack for finance to scam his away across the country.

Right then and there, we decided to partner up and strategize our next move over breakfast at a 24-hour diner across the street.

"Got any numbers on you?"

"I'll calculate one while we're eating."

That sealed the deal.

Over breakfast, he showed me four fake IDs in his possession—they were credible likenesses of him. I showed him one I had, a real driver's license that bore no resemblance to me, and another with my photo, which was an irregular foreign ID that I was not comfortable using. With his abundance of convincing alter egos, we settled on roles: I would be the administrator who set up the hotel authorization codes, since I could use someone else's ID in absentia, while leveraging the brand assets I had already created for a company that I wanted to start; he would be the front, using his multitude of IDs at check-in, while manually generating active numbers for me to use on the credit card authorization forms.

But our promising partnership would last only as long as the breakfast. The cashier wouldn't allow him to enter numbers into the point-of-sale terminal manually, so the plethora of generated numbers that he calculated by hand, no matter how much of a credit line they might have held, were useless. We decided to dine and dash—turns out that particular this 24-hour diner had been taken by dines-and-dashes so often that the manager had a direct line to the SeaTac cops who patrolled the area.

The cops caught up with us fewer than three blocks down the road. The police car swerved into the driveway to cut us off. The cop checked my ID first. I wasn't worried, as, at the time, I had never been arrested. The cop waiting with us said that he might just write me a ticket, but then his partner called him over for a discussion—my erstwhile partner-in-crime's ID (his real one) was associated with multiple felony warrants in Texas.

Both of us were taken to the Regional Justice Center (RJC) in Kent. People in the know refer to the jail as "RJ Suites" because every cell is single occupancy, complete with its own toilet. If you're going to jail for a lengthy period, that's the preferred destination.

While my would-be partner and I were in the common area, he intimated that a part of him was relieved that he got nabbed—it was time to return to Texas. He would have to stay in jail until the extradition procedures could be finalized. I, on the other hand, was arraigned the next day. It was nothing like I had imagined, held in a room with a bank of video monitors, my public defender barely conferred with me, as I had no criminal record at the time, so he asked the presiding judge, whose face appeared on the monitor in front of the chairs in which I and my public defender sat next to each other.

I was released on personal recognizance (PR'd) within a few hours. A court date was set for my sentencing, but I never showed up because the summons was sent to my address on record, which I had quit months ago.

* * *

IDENTITY THEFT IN THE SECOND DEGREE | FELONY | KING COUNTY SUPERIOR COURT

I felt invincible after being released from jail so quickly.

I unabashedly returned to my old haunt, SeaTac Airport, where I could pretend to be a cool nerd, working on my laptop while waiting for my flight. When I used to travel for business in my previous life, I liked to get to the airport about five hours early, giving myself time to catch up/finish up work that I had let pile up, buy myself food and drinks on the company charge card, snort all the loose cocaine I had on me (that I hadn't stuffed in gelatin capsules and stored in a prescription bottle to enjoy at my destination), and give myself enough time to take a luxurious shit before boarding the plane.

I was on the arrivals level, behind a long stand-up desk facing one of the baggage carousels, with my laptop open and flanked by real business travelers on both sides. Then, the far wall on the other side of the carousels magically opened, from which two Port of Seattle cops emerged. I wasn't doing anything wrong and trusted that my crisp, recently boosted attire and recent jail shower allowed me to blend in, so I wasn't worried. As the two cops came closer, I still wasn't concerned, until they stopped right in front of me. Port of Seattle Policeman #1 raised a blurry print of me in another part of the airport, holding onto a backpack next to a man sleeping on a row of chairs.

"Does this look familiar? Identification, please. May I search your bag?" Port of Seattle Policeman #1 demanded.

I was too stunned to say anything. So, I didn't. I didn't know what else to do, so I handed him my backpack and fished my ID from my brand-new Prada card wallet. Even though the well-heeled business travelers around me kept their heads down on their laptops, I felt all eyes on me. As Port of Seattle Policeman #1 searched my backpack, Port of Seattle Policeman #2 kept a watchful eye on me. My heart sank lower and lower with each incriminating item that Port of Seattle Policeman #1 retrieved from my backpack to showcase to the captive audience:

- A spiral notebook with a detailed record of the online accounts, emails, and passwords of the sleeping man whose backpack I had stolen, along with his social security number scribbled at the top of the page.
- The same man's checkbook.
- The same man's temporary Mexican consular identification card.
- A copy of the same Mexican national identification card with my photo expertly transposed on it.
- A debit card from a local credit union issued to the same man.

About a month before this incident, I was walking around the airport late at night, on my way to the smoking section to look for snipes (half-smoked cigarettes—smoking travelers always leave healthy snipes because they're bored, stressed, and in a hurry). I spotted a handful of people camped out in an area with banks of seats. An older couple was lying perpendicular to each other, and the man had his backpack on the floor at his feet. I snatched the backpack and walked away as quickly as my desire to look casual allowed.

What a find! This Boomer had no idea of the rules surrounding the security of his identity. Equally, the insecure format of his Mexican consular identification card was unparalleled—about the same size as an index card, with the person's details and photo seemingly photocopied onto it in black and white ink. To this day, I haven't been able to find it on the internet, but it was legitimate.

When the printing office opened the following day, I went to work—photocopied my driver license, cut out my photo (which was about the same size as the one on the man's ID), pasted it over the man's photo on the flimsy Mexican consular ID, scanned the jury-rigged document as an image, imported it into PowerPoint, erased the signature, saved it as a PDF, opened it in Acrobat, used the Fill & Sign feature to sign on the signature line, printed the doctored PDF on semi-heavy paper, cut the print-out into official size with a guillotine, and then stuck it in my pocket to give it a bit of weathering.

Next, I visited the Federal Way supercenter to conduct some social engineering. I hadn't shaved in a while, so my beard was longer than usual, revealing its progressive graying; I went to the bathroom, took my baseball cap off to show the equally progressing gray hair on my head, and washed my face, confirming in the mirror that my eyes were still puffy from no sleep over the past couple of days. I had to appear like a man in his mid-60s with a baby face, but that wasn't too difficult, as Mexicans and Filipinos often look younger than their chronological age.

I approached the electronics counter, put on my best rendition of a Mexican national who spent equal time in both countries (just a hint of an accent), and asked the cashier if I could use a check to pay for that laptop…over there, pointing to one behind the cashier's head. She confirmed that paying by check was allowed, but noted that the system sometimes wouldn't accept certain checks. Pushing my luck, I selected two $50 gift cards from an assortment below the counter, reminding myself to avoid purchasing too many, lest my purchase trigger a fraud alert. I asked the cashier to wait just one moment while I hurriedly picked out a phone with service and added it to my purchase. I wrote the check and showed her my "identification." She barely paused before slipping the check through the cash register system.

We awaited the results. The register just sat there for a few interminable seconds, processing, and then, BINGO—it went through.

Next stop: a cafe.

I hadn't had a laptop or phone in my possession since I had fallen out for hours in some dude's car in Everett. He and his buddy abruptly woke me up, told me some unintelligible story about needing me to wait for them in a fast-food restaurant, and with my mind fuzzy from perhaps an hour of sleep after days awake, I obeyed their instructions. As I sat at a table with the cup of coffee that the dude graciously bought for me, my mind started to clear—he had a strange look on his face when he said goodbye, as if guilt-ridden, and that's when I realized that they had left with my backpack and phone still in the car.

Now, with a lovely grande-almond-milk-peppermint-white-mocha-no-whip-cream-only-two-pumps-of-each-sweetener, thanks to one gift card, in front of me, I went through the process of setting up a hotel room. I chose a three-star hotel (didn't want to push my luck with four-star paranoia) in Auburn (the hotels on the Highway got hit with more scams than any other area, so I would occasionally venture farther afield to hit more fertile ground).

In the hotel room that night, with a fresh bag of crystallized confidence, I went to work monetizing the Boomer's identity traces. As I expected, none of the passwords for his online accounts were still valid—those are the first things, along with credit cards, that people shut down after a theft.

Having been turned away from what should have been the first order of business had I had a phone or laptop at hand, I turned to his Social Security number, which was scribbled in the notebook, and his checkbook, which provided his address. I needed a way to cash those checks without going to a check-cashing facility. Unless you have an established account, those places, notorious for preying on the poor, are hit or miss. Plus, I didn't want to show my face and risk getting added to a fraud alert algorithm.

I hatched a strategy to open a local credit union checking account in the Boomer's name and deposit his checks. When opening accounts online, the verification system poses questions based on your historical records, typically including the names of relatives, previous addresses, and old phone numbers. I looked up the Boomer's name on a people search app, using a gift card to pay for a full year of the premium subscription, which gave me access to deep historical records. I saw that one of his previous addresses was local—that's the one I would use to open the account.

I kept my phone beside me while applying for a new checking account so that I could refer to the public records information during the validation process. BINGO—the success page instructed me to visit a local branch to pick up my (his) new debit card.

I messaged all my street folks. But that's the thing about getting a room away from the Highway—no one over there wants to trek far away. It's so much more convenient to step out of your hotel and run into people in the streets or on the all-night A Line bus. I didn't know many folks in Auburn, and I'm not one of those who feel comfortable inviting just anyone to my room. Two casinos were in the same city, but that was a journey with no night buses.

I took drugs on my own for the next couple of days, while ordering room service and nibbling at it. The following Monday, I visited a local credit union branch and successfully picked up "my" new debit card using the flimsy, doctored identification. I deposited one of the Boomer's checks, feeling like an inducted member of the Anonymous worldwide hacker collective, that is, before the SeaTac Airport incident.

After searching my backpack, Port of Seattle Policeman #1 cuffed me while reading my rights. The polite crowd around me couldn't keep their heads down on their laptops any longer. Both Port of Seattle cops led me through the hidden door in the far wall.

Then they bundled me up the stairs to the internal police station. That place had to be the most well-appointed police station in all of Seattle, on par with what I imagine a well-funded federal crime agency might look like. Port of Seattle Policeman #2 was cataloging my stuff—he paused over my new Prada card wallet, putting it near his nose to sniff at it, and then holding it weirdly to his lips before placing it on his desk.

After napping in a holding cell for I don't know how long, I was summarily transported back to RJ Suites. Once booked and processed, I was placed in the same cell where I had stayed two days ago. Famished, I made my way down to the common area for dinner. My erstwhile running partner was there, still awaiting his extradition to Texas.

"You're not a very good criminal." These were the only words he said to me during my two-day detention.

I appeared in court and, again, was PR'd. When the officer returned my property, I went through my backpack and wasn't surprised to find that my laptop and other incriminating items had been confiscated. At least, they had compassionately left this homeless man his phone. I fished my driver's license from the bottom of my backpack, but the brand-new Prada card wallet was nowhere to be found.

***

POSSESSION OF STOLEN PROPERTY IN THE SECOND DEGREE | FELONY | KITSAP COUNTY SUPERIOR COURT

A gentle hand shook me awake.

As the sleep fog slowly lifted, I realized I had fallen off in front of a slot machine. The micro-movements of slot machines—similar to the fine motor movements required in thumbing a text or rolling a loose-leaf cigarette—have a way of lulling sleep-deprived addicts. A hand shaking me awake usually meant that a casino security guard had caught me fallen out.

This time, it was Charlotte—she was Ava's best friend; we ended up developing a close friendship after Ava and I split for good, as she knew about Ava's ongoing tryst with Pablo, and had tried desperately to make me open my eyes without breaking her loyalty to Ava.

"C'mon. Let's get outta here."

I was so happy to see Charlotte's face; her gentle command made me feel safe.

Charlotte experienced one of the roughest childhoods I'd ever heard of—ritualistically abused by her older brother, who was subjected to the same rituals that he meted out to her; she and her siblings passed through one abusive foster home after another; miraculously, an older couple adopted all of the siblings together, but the damage had been done. Charlotte used alcohol and drugs to diminish the emotional pain that she had never been taught to recognize and process, and she committed crimes to lash out at a system that had failed her.

Charlotte's acts of systemic rebellion offered a high in and of themselves, as addictive as substances. She was sent to the Peninsula's version of Orange Is the New Black at the tender age of 19 and came to live with me and Ava on Bainbridge Island after she was released from Purdy Prison. She possessed the intelligence to commit financial scams that even I couldn't pull off. Charlotte was my street daughter—a chip off the old block.

As smart as Charlotte was, the success of the mission on which we were about to embark would be all down to her boyfriend, who was waiting in his car for us in the parking lot. Still half-asleep, I stumbled into his backseat.

Before Charlotte found me slumped in front of the slot machine, I had been awake for nearly one week. But I had run out of drugs and lost my last $10 on the slot machine that then had hypnotized me to sleep.

I must have fallen out while riding in the backseat of her boyfriend's car because, when I initially got into the car, it was dawn, and when I came to, I was alone in the car parked at the Poulsbo Walmart, the sun high in the sky. It didn't take long for Charlotte and her boyfriend to return with a cart-full of stuff. My booster mind knew that this wasn't a run-of-the-mill shoplifting trip: the items included electronics usually kept securely behind the sales counter or locked up in their respective aisles.

I felt like a kid on Christmas Day.

They finished loading the car, and Charlotte's boyfriend started backing out.

"He was up a lotta money before we found you at the casino, and then he lost it all. He was so mad. When you fell out back there, we drove to Bainbridge. Something told him that a car parked in this one driveway had something good in it. The guy left his wallet!" Charlotte couldn't contain her excitement.

"I wanna go shopping."

"Here, take this," she said in her best suburban mom voice while handing me a credit card. "We'll be back"

I took the credit card, got out of the car, and went into the store, making a beeline for the electronics section. I hadn't lost my phone yet, so my strategy to stay under the radar of the fraud alert system was to pick out a cheap laptop and nothing else. But the credit card was declined. I asked the sales associate to try again. Nothing. I felt a little betrayed. But then, I reminded myself that Charlotte and her boyfriend had the other cards on them, so there was still hope of cashing out when they returned for me.

I waited at one of the parking lot entrances away from the store. Within 20 minutes, a car screeched to a halt right in front of me. An angry middle-aged man swung his door open, confronting me from the protective vantage of his passenger seat. A younger man, undoubtedly his son, was driving.

"You're a thief. The police are on their way."

The police car was already in sight, weaving its way through the parking lot.

"I don't know what you're talking about." I looked at Mr. Aggrieved with a straight face.

Mr. Aggrieved's suburban courage precluded any notions of getting himself out of his car and confronting me, an accused criminal, so I inched my way to a nearby bush to surreptitiously drop his credit card.

A cop got out of the car and approached me. "Hello, sir. We're responding to a security call about fraudulent use of a credit card."

Whether or not the incriminating evidence was on me or wedged in a nearby bush, I knew I'd be toast when the cop ran my ID and saw a litany of my recent charges.

"My credit card!" Mr. Aggrieved pouted from the comfort of his car's passenger seat.

"Sir, we'll handle this." The cop turned and held up a printout of me standing at the Walmart electronics sales counter. "This was taken about 30 to 45 minutes ago in that store. And then this man called to tell us that someone who looked like the perpetrator was standing where you are." The cop then looked at the printout and then back at me. "But I think the person in the photo has a darker complexion than you do, if you don't mind my saying. Sorry to bother you, sir," the cop added in his most DEI tone.

And that was it. For real—I was let go. Mr. Aggrieved was livid and threw a tantrum in his passenger seat. But he wouldn't look back at me, overcome by his Bainbridge Island fear of homeless criminal drug addicts.

I wouldn't have attempted any violence. I was just abandoned, with nowhere to call home, and needing my fix.

I texted Charlotte.

ME: "Don't come back."

Kitsap County wasn't done with me—that incident would be used to build a felony case against me, which would be included in the spate of charges in my Drug Court charging document more than a year later.

However, being let go by the police allowed me to revisit that intoxicating feeling of invincibility.

* * *

THEFT OF A MOTOR VEHICLE | FELONY | KITSAP COUNTY SUPERIOR COURT

The first time I saw Chloe, she was washing her hair with water and combing it clean in front of a mirrored window of the supercenter in Bonney Lake. I stood there, so stunned by her appearance that I forgot to be self-conscious about staring at her. I could tell she was watching me watching her in the window.

I was waiting for my latest running partners, a couple, to finish boosting—we had met on the bus in Auburn; they were sitting in the seats in front of me, and we instantly understood that we were each other's people; they were on a mission to acquire goods to trade for drugs and were on their way to retrieve the boyfriend's car to drive to a well-to-do area for easy pickings. I offered my services as their accomplice.

I was smoking a cigarette near the car when Chloe had magically appeared.

Amongst the street population, I noticed that a higher percentage of preternaturally hot girls per capita seems to exist than in the general population. My theory is that their presence is too much for their families to handle, so they become the black sheep, ritualistically abused—sometimes physically, always emotionally—and are excommunicated in their early teens. The multifaceted abuse of their childhoods develops an avoidant attachment style, including problems with intimacy, investing little emotion in social and romantic relationships, and an unwillingness or inability to share thoughts and feelings with others. At the same time, their need to obtain resources, coupled with the facility to do so using their unearthly hotness, obligates them to give just enough attention to their suitors to keep them enthralled.

Women like Chloe were the perfect foil for my ambivalent attachment style, with my penchant for neediness countered by reluctance toward intimacy and vulnerability, consistent worry over inconsistent displays of affection, and a tendency to become distraught when relationships end. Chloe's unavailability felt familiar to me, so I confused it with affection. These varying levels of insecure attachment styles, learned in early childhood and cemented during adolescence, result from our caregivers' inability to provide the requisite amount of affection and attention children need to develop a sense of safety and security in the world.

Chloe and I both ended up on the streets, where our vulnerabilities heighten our insecurities, so we turn to each other for any semblance of security. Neither of us had the internal resources to provide what the other needed emotionally, so we sized each other up to determine whether we could deliver the emotional surrogates of drugs and sex.

That day in Bonney Lake, Chloe gave me her Facebook name. She finally messaged me when the guy who had been letting her squat at his place had become inpatient and started pushing hard for sex. All she wanted from him was a warm place to stay, but her technique involved playing on the attraction that men of some means, whether those means were sustainable or temporary, inevitably had for her. When the time came to keep the implicit promise of transactional sex, it then became time for her to dip and find a new resource. That time had arrived at the same time I temporarily borrowed a truck and acquired a few blue notes. Before our first date, I cruised the Highway to procure a stack of meth for me and some nice heroin for Chloe—better than flowers for courting a junkie.

With meth keeping me company, I stayed up until the momentous morning of our appointment, finding Chloe at our arranged pick-up spot in Sumner. She hopped in and I immediately handed her the bag of black designed to curry her favor.

"Aw, you shouldn't have. Well, you know you should have. Mind if I boof a little? I'm not tryna mix a shot while you're driving."

"Please do," I said in my most courtly manner.

Chloe broke off a healthy piece of the sticky black block and proceeded to stick it up her ass. That did it—love at first boof. That she performed this act within minutes of our meeting gave her an air of casual hippie gangster-ness that I found intoxicating. That single act got to me in the same way that watching a woman shoot up in a neck vein gets me. Female addicts who literally stun you with their attractiveness all seem to have problematic veins, challenging to find even for a phlebotomist doing it for legitimate reasons, so the vein-challenged resort to using the more explicit, and heretofore untouched, veins in their long, sensual necks rather than spending hours searching in vain for veins in their extremities.

The indulgent danger of such acts lends an eroticism that grabs me by the throat.

I handed a canister of wet wipes to Chloe—eroticism does not preclude hygiene.

We spent our first night under a bridge at the side of a lightly used road. Chloe was refreshingly upfront about our implicit arrangement—she'd be with me as long as I could provide drugs and shelter; in exchange, since there was mutual attraction, she would give me carnal comfort. I mixed up a meth shot for myself and asked Chloe to do the honors. Ever since Ava hit me just right, this exchange had become my litmus test to measure my true attraction to any new woman. Unfortunately, Chloe's manners in my hallowed ritual of surrogate love had an air of impersonality—her approach felt rote and distant; even the way she stuck the needle in my arm was a bit rough.

"Kiss?" Chloe's tone was less a question and more a demure demand after completing our ceremony.

Even with meth already rushing through me, her little love-peck felt a bit cold.

I was out of money, so I contacted Mimi, who lived in the area, to see if she was ready to be of use. She and I had been introduced a few weeks back by a mutual acquaintance who knew I was looking for an on-again-off-again business partner.

Hearing that I needed time to chase paper, Chloe arranged to spend the night with her mother and stepfather. How weird that she was still sufficiently connected with her parents while living on the streets that she would spend time with them—perhaps they were trying to show her tough love in their own misinformed way.

After I dropped Chloe off, I met up with Mimi—she was driving a late-model SUV and had an account at the check-cashing place, which seemed to clash with her otherwise respectable appearance, unless you understood that she was a tweaker. Mimi and I handled our business and split the proceeds.

"Text me when you want to do this again."

I detected an undercurrent of desperation in Mimi's tone, which I planned to use when I became desperate myself.

The next day, I met up with my little Chamorro brother. We first met when I spent a cold night at the Fife bus stop in front of a convenience store a block from a casino. As a younger fellow islander, he called me Kuya (older brother in Tagalog), which warmed my heart. Over breakfast, we made plans to meet his connection that afternoon at a nearby casino to get a really good deal on heroin—more flowers for Chloe's return. After giving him my last $100 to make the promised deal, he took the keys out of the ignition, put them in his pocket, and never returned.

Chloe's parents dropped her off. I told her what had happened. She was furious.

"I feel...I don't know...cheated, I guess, that you got drugs for yourself and not me. I RETURNED for you. I CAME BACK. And this is what I come back to?"

Part of me wanted her to leave so that I'd be free to prowl on my own. The codependent part of me felt responsible for her now, for the agreement that we sealed with a rough hit and a distant kiss. Desperate, I remembered Mimi's newfound usefulness. She proved to be a fellow codependent, starving for adrenaline-producing adventure. She might have a thing for me, which I could leverage. I called, not merely texted, but actually called her with the whole story.

Mimi arrived in 15 minutes. I gave her a big hug and a healthy shard of meth as a token of my appreciation. She whisked us back to her house.

Mimi was a young widow, likely in her 40s, with two teenage twin daughters. She and her husband got together when she was only 14 years old. He tried to expose her to the life events that he imagined she had missed by getting together with him at such an early age and marrying when she reached the age of consent, forcibly encouraging her to engage in little affairs.

When her husband died suddenly, Mimi was left rudderless, so she embarked on a second childhood, becoming the cool mom who molded her children into the two coolest, most popular girls in middle school by allowing the kids to use her garage as a weed-smoking den. In parallel, Mimi got into the meth scene, adopting the good-looking segment of the local homeless population. They ended up just using her, and she obliged.

Once we arrived at Mimi's respectable little four-bedroom rambler, she initially set me and Chloe up in the garage. Within a couple of days, Mimi and her lodger—an older man, probably my age, who was a used car salesman and her meth connection—had a falling-out, so it didn't take long for Chloe and me to attain favorite homeless-peeps status, a distinction that came with the spare bedroom. I had a feeling Mimi and her lodger had an affair going sour, and Chloe and I arrived when the affair was bottoming out. Whatever the case, Chloe and I felt like we'd been gifted this arrangement, as it was nearing the holiday season.

"Look. I know my place. I need to play second fiddle to Mimi if she's gonna let us stay here. I give you permission to spend more time with her. I won't get jealous. It's cold outside." Chloe smiled to emphasize that last point.

Mimi and I spent hours devising and implementing financial scams. We kept hitting dead ends.

One night, I persuaded her to let me borrow her car to go farther afield, trekking back to Bainbridge Island, which provided more potential ROI than any of our failed scams: keys to a late-model Mercedes-Benz.

But cash flow remained dry. Regardless of the loot's inherent value, liquidation was problematic. Chloe had a habit of going away to get drugs from this older guy she'd known for years, someone who adored her and gave her drugs when she was down and out. She was obliged to stay with her fan for a few days, her mere presence as payment. I felt emasculated every time. To make the heroin gift last longer, Chloe would spend all her time in the bedroom, getting just high enough to barely cure her sickness, then allowing herself to get slightly sicker before administering a tad of medicine.

Chloe's constant teetering on the verge of deliberate sickness created a natural barrier to surrogate-intimacy. Erecting another barrier was my required presence in the general living area, playing the male Chloe role for Mimi. That's what platonic street whores pay to get out from the cold.

"It's been over a month now. Almost two." Mimi approached me near the end of our stay with the forced bravado of a people-pleaser who uses anger to set boundaries. "This isn't working."

"I have that key to my old neighbor's Mercedes. I just need a ride there." I pulled my get-out-of-jail card from my back pocket.

"Where will you keep it?"

"I'll park it somewhere in the neighborhood, unhook the battery to disable the GPS, and then you push it with your car into the garage." It was the worst strategy ever, but we were that desperate.

Mimi agreed.

That very night, we drove two hours to Bainbridge Island. As we approached the Agate Pass Bridge, Mimi noticed the casino on the right.

"Whaaaaat? It's beautiful."

"I'll meet you there," I said in my coolest tone.

One of my old neighbors owned the car I was about to steal. I didn't know their names. I had waved to them numerous times, but I make it a habit NOT to get to know my neighbors. I keep to myself. At that moment, my habit allowed me to depersonalize them.

Word of advice: Never, ever, steal a car on an island with only two ways out—a ferry crossing and a bridge.

When I arrived at the bridge driving my ex-neighbor's Mercedes-Benz, six police cars were waiting on the other side, blocking one lane of the highway and the casino entrance.

The cops cuffed my hands behind my back and forced me to my knees. As I watched cars roll slowly by in one lane, the gravel piercing my knees, I caught Mimi's car. She kept her gaze straight ahead.

I would spend a week in the Kitsap County Jail in Port Orchard. After that, I was released on personal recognizance, with my arraignment set for a date I wouldn't remember. As with all my pending charges, the court summons would be sent to my old Bainbridge Island address, where I had just stolen my innocent neighbor's car. I'd miss the court date, as per usual.

Upon my release, I managed to get in touch with Chloe. She had hooked up with a married couple on the brink of divorce—they gave her drugs and shelter in exchange for being their "third" (promised but consummation never guaranteed).

Mimi had kicked Chloe out after the fanfare of my arrest spooked her. She told Chloe that she was done with The Life. So, the rent I had paid for me and Chloe to stay in Mimi's house for nearly two months wasn't merely an inconsistent supply of meth and my platonic whoredom.

For Christmas, I gave Mimi the gift of scaring her straight.

Chapter 6

Sleepless at Wally's

Imagine a gaggle of homeless people—cold, hungry, and dope sick—carrying backpacks full of their soiled belongings, with nowhere to go. They walk into a big box retailer and are instantly crushed by the gratuitous abundance of it all. How could national retailers sell everything in their stores? They can't. That's not the point. The point is to give consumers a choice.

To achieve this goal, big box retailers stock multiple orders of magnitude more products than they can sell. This strategy involves disposing of and incinerating 40% of their produce and any non-canned consumer packaged goods, as well as discarding or reselling for pennies on the dollar a significant portion of the 30% of all items sold that are eventually returned.

Our gaggle of homeless people isn't aware of any of this. But they can feel it. And this feeling creates the notion that, with all the money big box retailers make, they surely won't miss a tent, sleeping bag, flashlight, hoodie, food, and maybe a pair of earbuds nice enough to trade for some dope.

Patrolling the parking lots from early evening until the midnight hours are concerned neighborhood watchers. They use their block's Facebook page or NextDoor app to keep tabs on the most prolific shoplifters, whose shenanigans bleed into the nearby neighborhoods.

The neighbors take turns parking in vacant lots that are notorious gathering places for homeless addicts to take their drugs out of sight. These upstanding folks in their late-model cars provide free loss prevention and property security services to the big retailers because they: 1) Want to keep public spaces safe and sanitary from used hypodermic needles and discarded packaging from boosted goods; and 2) Believe they're helping big box retailers keep the price of goods from increasing due to theft.

Approximately one percent of big retailers' annual revenues go out the door due to shoplifting, organized retail theft, and primarily to employee theft. These economic elephants have access to state-of-the-art facial recognition technology, as well as high-definition cameras throughout the store to track anyone looking suspicious, which are then broadcast to an array of video monitors in the in-store mission control of their loss prevention team.

The combined efforts of an entire industry to curb retail theft have still resulted in continued annual increases in shrinkage (inventory loss). Spending more than half the monetary value of shrinkage on loss prevention makes no economic sense for the big retailers, so they accept this loss as a cost of doing business.

This is the scene I entered after spending two weeks in RJ Suites, where a warrant was issued for missing my court date on the identity theft charge at SeaTac Airport. The COVID lockdown had just been implemented. The streets were lawless. It felt like the apocalypse well and truly happened.

The first place I headed was the supercenter in North Federal Way. An associate stopped me at the door, instructing me to put on a mask before entering the store. You want me to wear a mask? Man, I was about to take just a few things that I needed after getting out of jail, but now, under the cloak of a surgical mask, I'm taking anything I please.

I was on the streets full-time now. The hotels had banned me. The night managers at even the seediest motels had seen too much of me. Without access to the resources I once had, I naturally gravitated towards areas near large retailers, public amenities, public land, and a community of like-minded folks. No area in the Pacific Northwest embodies these traits as comprehensively as the Highway—the nickname for Highway 99, cutting down King County from Everett to Fife.

I became entrenched in The Life: wide-scale organized retail theft, private property crime, unmanageable trash, and unsanitary and unsafe public spaces. We who made the Highway our home slammed and smoked and snorted our drugs at bus stops, alleyways behind buildings, and in the back rows of the all-night buses because we had nowhere else to take our medicine. We left used syringes and discarded packaging for the food we had stolen and eaten, and the new clothes we had boosted and changed into every few days, wherever they may fall, because we had no designated garbage cans of our own that we could wheel out to the curb every Tuesday to get picked up.

Nobody in the surrounding neighborhoods gave a shit about us, so why give a shit about them?

However, I couldn't completely operate on such a sentiment during the early days of the COVID lockdown, as neighbors started caring for one another, regardless of whether they owned a house nearby. One of the social-engineering ploys that I often used to shoplift entailed stuffing my pockets and backpack full of items, get in line with a few items in hand like a real paying customer, use a debit card that I had in my possession but which I knew was invalid, and pretend to intend to pay for the items. When the card would inevitably be declined, I'd feign surprise and then walk out looking dejected, but with my pockets and backpack brimming.

But what I didn't expect was the communal altruism during the nascent COVID lockdown foiling my plans. The person in line behind me often offered to pay for my purchase. My heart of hearts exploded at the caring gesture, while my dark heart immediately identified a new string I could pull. This pandemic-inspired altruism and societal bonding made my social-engineering ploy that much more effective, arousing the cashier's sympathy and giving me further permission to walk out of the store unassumingly, with items in hand that the person behind me had donated, while my pockets and backpack stayed criminally jam-packed.

The retailers themselves got in on the act. Rumor had it that the North Federal Way Walmart loss prevention staff offered an intermittent social program with the help of the onsite McDonald's—they would provide free food to the hungry homeless boosters known to descend en masse upon Walmart during dinner time. Granted, it was a sound investment—the ad hoc program deterred retail theft, while the cost of the free food would be an order of magnitude less than the value of potential stolen goods. Still, it was a kind gesture.

There are two archetypes of street people: Panhandlers on one side and Hustlers on the other. The former are mainly law-abiding and dependent, while the latter are criminals and ferociously independent (though the latter still depend on the lightly guarded surplus of a wasteful society).

I was a card-carrying hustler and looked down my nose at panhandlers, setting up camp for hours at stoplights, flying their signs written with entreaties for help, while donning their most helpless expressions to elicit the sympathy of the drivers trapped in their cars at intersections. I refused to lower myself to groveling to the "almost-haves" of the world, denying them the opportunity to leverage my misfortune for a little respite from their not-quite-middle-class guilt.

I would rather take what I wanted. There's more than enough to go around. I was merely redistributing wealth in a corrupt capitalist system that needed to be blown up anyway, which is what I told myself every time I stole from national retailers, misused credit cards I found while car prowling, or debit cards that someone had mindlessly left in an ATM. I even managed to justify car prowling—the insurance companies, the biggest racket in the history of rackets, were the real entities from which I was ultimately stealing.

But the COVID lockdown gave me a reason to implicitly implore the sympathy of the "almost-have" behind me in the checkout line and the national retailers assuaging their guilt while helping their bottom line.

* * *

Like dung beetles following a herd of elephants, a gaggle of homeless people gathered in a grassy area at the far end of the parking lot in the Renton retail center anchored by big box retailers.

Harry was holding court, as he did. A faction of street folks saw him as the king of the homeless. But a ruling majority ridiculed him as crazy because of the outlandish personal story that he would tell anyone who would listen, especially women, some of whom he successfully enchanted with his story, persuading them into sucking his cock in one of the many portable toilets stationed near public spaces during the COVID era.

The first time I met Harry was at a motel popular with fully and semi-homeless people in SeaTac. I was staying in a room with a Mexican prostitute and her two guys, one of whom had remembered me from one of my stints at the SCORE jail. I had been running with the two Mexican guys for a while, but our run hadn't been as profitable as we had all hoped, so the partnership was on its last legs. The prostitute had left the room for a smoke, and when the length of her absence crossed the threshold of a normal cigarette break, the SCORE Mexican got antsy. He asked me to check out what she was up to—he didn't want to do it himself, wanting to avoid looking like he cared. Since he had paid for the room with the proceeds from selling boosted steaks and seafood to a couple of migrant Mexican families staying at the motel, I obliged.

Walking around the property, I eventually spotted the prostitute talking with a white dude—long hair, confident, probably around my age, but in decent shape. The prostitute seemed coy around him. I stopped, threw my cigarette on the ground, and stepped on it, signaling that I knew what she was up to.

"Arnel, this is Harry." The prostitute turned around and introduced me to her friend.

Harry raised his chin slightly, signaling acknowledgment. "If you ever need anything…black, clear, whatever."

I vaguely nodded and kept walking, heading back to the room.

The next day, I was walking down the Highway at the Tukwila end. At first, I didn't recognize the guy approaching me, limping down the road carrying a handful of DeWalt power tools.

"Remember me? From the motel last night," Harry stopped me mid-stride. "I'm about to go to my sister's, just up the road. Tryna trade these tools to my brother-in-law for some clear. He's a dealer. Walk with me."

I was already in mid-thought about how and where to get that night's fix, so it didn't take much to persuade me. Throughout the COVID lockdown, Harry and I would make this journey countless times, and I'd become a trusted customer of his dealer-brother-in-law. But on this inaugural visit, I waited outside while he made the deal—it's bad manners to bring someone new, unannounced, to your plug's abode.

When Harry returned, he treated me to a big fat line of meth. It instantly purchased my loyalty, at least until he ran out or something about him made me wary. We walked around—well, I walked, and he limped, as his new Lebron Airs hurt his feet.

"I asked around about you." Harry kept his gaze straight ahead.

"What'd you hear?" I sized him up.

"That you're new, used to be a professional, good booster. I'm looking for a partner to run with." Harry stopped at an empty bus stop shelter in front of the 24-hour grocery store, produced a nice-sized bag of meth, picked out a shard, took a dollar bill out of his pocket, folded it in half, placed the shard in the crease, folded the bill over horizontally, closed the ends vertically to create an efficient little package, pulled a Bic lighter from his other pocket, placed the package onto the bus bench, and crushed up into a fine, fat line, handing the finished package to me, along with a rolled-up bill to use as a tooter.

I was intrigued. I had grown accustomed to people, both men and women, propositioning a partnership. I made a good front—the way I looked, my manner of speaking, my table manners. Equally, these would-be business partners always had some stature and means on the streets—they were highly visible and had a reputation for getting things done. These partnerships were always on and off, fizzling out and then resuming when we'd happen upon each other down the road. But Harry's story, which he told me as we walked around for miles that night, was different, though familiar.

One of Harry's parents was part of the Chicago Gotti family. Both of his parents were killed for some mafia-related reason. Only five years old (the same age my parents moved our family from the Philippines to the U.S.), Harry was shipped off to live with his aunt and uncle in Seattle. He took to living on the streets at an early age, joining the Crips and selling drugs, all the while getting good grades and being a star athlete in football, basketball, and baseball, activities that offered year-round safety from the streets and comfort in a warm court or locker room. Harry was drafted by the Los Angeles Angels organization in the 1990s. I once looked him up to corroborate this claim, but I couldn't find him in any of the major league rosters at the time, so I tried looking at the affiliated minor league teams, but there were too many players to sift through—he made his millions, though an injury had cut his career short.

Harry returned to the Seattle area, bought a house, and resumed selling drugs. Weed was his cash cow before its legalization. The most intriguing part of this chapter of his story is that his home became a revolving-door domicile for a segment of the street population. Harry housed them, not out of altruism, but as a well-appointed trap house. Then, the Feds caught up with him and raided his home, tearing down the drywall to expose his money stash. He spent years in prison, taken care of by his people on the inside, and eventually struck a deal to pay a few million to the Feds in exchange for reduced prison time.

Harry's D.O.C. oversight had finally concluded a couple of months before we met. He immediately took to the streets, going on multi-day expeditions before eventually dragging himself back to his house near the Renton Highlands when he was well past the point of falling out. Harry had a talent for somehow finding his way home in the worst state of falling out. He claimed to have economic interests in a truck dealership in Kent and a porn website, waiting until the Feds' watchful eyes eased up a bit before dipping into those funds. Harry and I would lose each other on the streets for weeks at a time—usually, I'd be in jail; he, on the other hand, would be back at home recuperating. Sometimes, he'd forewarn me that he'd be gone for a week or two on a gang-related economic mission.

There are a handful of activities, along with their adjacent undertakings, in which adrenaline junkies participate during week-long vacations—mountain climbing, skydiving, surfing, and hunting. Harry took the streets for homeless benders.

I decided to believe most of Harry's story. Just as I'd mostly believed Aiden for the same reason. After running together for a few months, I asked Harry if he knew Aiden.

"Denny? He gets too high. He's a liability now. You know he stole his story from one of the guys in Miami?"

I wasn't sure what to believe. There was at least a grain of truth on both sides. Either way, Harry's open secret was safe with me.

Back at the Renton retail center parking lot, one of the homeless guys pulled away from the flock and approached me, out of Harry's earshot. "That guy's crazy. Why're you hanging out with him?"

"Why don't you say that to Harry's face?" I threw my cigarette to the ground.

The homeless guy slinked away.

Seven o'clock is the witching hour for homeless boosters. If you know what to look for, you can see an interspersed procession walking at a zombie's pace through the parking lot of any superstore in an attempt to appear as natural as possible. The witching hour signaled dinner time for homeless boosters and their customers, so it was time to steal something to munch on and something else of value to trade for drugs or cash.

Customers of ill-gotten goods usually came in the form of the following categories:

- Korean and Mexican families who valued high-priced consumer goods sold at the desperate discounts that only booster-addicts could provide
- Cartel members who regularly traded drugs for consumer goods at an even steeper discount
- Run-of-the-mill addicts who have a nice stash of drugs that night and might be interested in a cool tactical flashlight or the latest Adidas backpack.

"I'm about to fall off, man." Harry's eyes were out of sync, and he teetered as he stood.

I had crashed out for a couple of hours here and there during this excursion with Harry, but he had stayed up the entire time, keeping sentry when I'd fall off.

"Ok, let's make one more hit, get some cash, and see your brother-in-law. Then I'll get you back to your house." I needed more drugs.

Harry's respite would have to wait.

The last time we visited Harry's brother-in-law to trade, he made it clear that he would need cash next time.

Another one of the homeless boosters on the grassy area told Harry that he had a direct line to a few Korean guys whose wives wanted a specific brand of baby formula for their newborn babies. The Korean community seemed to own a large swath of south King County, especially around Federal Way, and many appreciated economic loopholes.

"They'll buy as much of that type of baby formula for half the retail price," the homeless booster exclaimed, showing off his credentials to Harry. "But I can't go into that store without LP (loss prevention staff) all over me."

Half the retail price was an unusual take, as street prices, such as those on Craigslist, are typically no more than one-third of retail.

"Arnel can do it. We'll give you a cut if you can hook us up to your customers," Harry slurred.

"Him?" The homeless booster sized me up, underestimating me.

"Yeah. Him," Harry boasted.

"What's the name of that baby formula again?" I directed my question at Harry, ignoring the homeless booster.

I gave my backpack to Harry for safekeeping, knowing that walking into any store with a backpack immediately tips off the loss prevention team. As I approached the store, I decided to use my sneakiest and most elegant social-engineering ploy. Unlike clumsy boosters, I didn't like the sloppiness of smash and dash—hurrying out of the store with stolen goods and setting off the alarm. I preferred a smooth approach—getting what I came for and walking out undetected, like a regular paying customer. This method only works if you walk in carrying nothing and are dressed respectably. I had boosted new clothes the day before, and the weather had been relatively pleasant for the cusp of late winter-early spring, so I looked the part. The elegant boosting style I preferred meant I had won the game on multiple levels. And make no mistake—boosting is a zero-sum game.

Once inside the store, I retrieved a shopping cart from the row near the entrance. I sauntered over to the sporting goods department and picked out a smart Adidas duffel bag, the only one on the shelves that hadn't been marked with a security tag. I placed it in the shopping cart, and as I slowly pushed the cart toward the aisle where the baby formula was located, I unzipped the duffel bag and positioned it at the bottom of the cart. When I arrived at the shelves of baby formula, I noticed that the brand preferred by young, monied Korean mothers was on the bottom shelf. There were 16 remaining, so I took all of them. I resumed pushing the shopping cart while placing the canisters in the duffel bag whenever I arrived at a spot between the aisles that seemed out of sight from security cameras. Before reaching the customer service desk, I zipped the duffel bag closed.

"Can I help you?" the woman at the customer service desk asked, her words muffled behind her surgical mask.

"Yes, I need to return all this baby formula. I purchased everything you had a couple days ago, but my wife said I got the wrong brand. These are expensive." I shook my head in mock exasperation, then took the cannisters from the duffel bag and placed them on the counter..

"Do you have the receipt?" The customer service clerk's eyes smiled ever so slightly.

"I don't. My wife has it with her. I just remembered when I pulled into the parking lot," I said.

"I'm sorry, sir. We need a receipt for your refund," the customer service clerk apologized.

"That sucks. She's gonna be mad at me. Can I exchange these for the brand she wants?"

"We really need a receipt." The customer service clerk was pleasant but firm.

"Ok," I tried to say dejectedly, but not too dejected. I began placing the cannisters back into the duffel bag. Then I took the bag out of the shopping cart. "Can I just leave this here?" I asked, motioning to the cart.

The customer service clerk paused for a moment, staring at me. Her eyes were no longer pleasantly half-smiling. She realized that she'd just been had, seeming to purse her lips behind her mask. She gave me a slight nod, one that appeared to be performed against her will.

I started walking toward the door through which I had entered. The automatic glass door swung open. I walked through it, and when I didn't hear the alarm sound, I stopped just beyond the security sensors, slowly looking left and right, like a gunslinger who had just gunned down an enemy at high noon, and then proceeded to stroll back toward the congregation.

"No go?"

"They only had 16 cannisters left, so I took them all." I threw the duffle bag at the homeless booster's feet.

The homeless booster looked at me, then crouched down and unzipped the bag.

"Wow. How the hell did you do that?"

"I told you," Harry mumbled from a nearby bus bench where he had camped out.

I picked up the duffel bag, walked to the bus bench, and placed it next to Harry.

"I didn't get to pick up anything to eat since I was focused on the loot. You stay here. I'm going to that Chinese place right there to try out this credit card I found. Don't move." I patted Harry on the shoulder.

The credit card didn't work.

Harry and the duffel bag were gone when I returned to the bus bench. I tried texting him, but no answer. I knew he wouldn't scam me like that. Still, I struggled to find an explanation until I ran into him again a couple of weeks later. Harry explained that he had been so out of it that he allowed the homeless booster to put him on a bus to Southcenter. The homeless booster said that I had instructed him to do so. Luckily, one of Harry's allies found him slumped on a bus bench at the Southcenter Transit Center, where the homeless booster had left him. Harry's ally sent him home in an Uber.

The homeless booster ultimately acquired the entire supply of baby formula preferred by young, discerning Korean mothers.

*　*　*

For as long as I was on the streets during the COVID lockdown, I never encountered one homeless person throughout my wide-ranging circles who contracted the virus. Not a single soul. While everyone in polite society was cooped up in their houses, talking to each other on Zoom and wearing masks wherever they went—even some of y'all so germ-freaked out that you're wearing masks in your car—us street folks were strolling through buses with our masks on our chins, only putting them on or up when entering stores. Deserted by genteel civilization, we were abandoned to the fresh air day and night, without a care in the world (other than that one overwhelming need to get our daily fix, somehow, someway).

The streets were lawlessly ours, and at some level, so were the stores—people had been warned to distance themselves from each other, and this command engendered a paranoia that begat a policy of store employees allowing masked homeless boosters to get away with shoplifting unencumbered and unmolested in the early days of the lockdown. However, once the retail sector tallied the costs of such pervasive paranoia, making up for having missed their almighty revenue targets became a higher priority than halting the spread of the virus.

Government representatives beholden to national retailers recruited local police to chase down homeless boosters who had already left stores with stolen goods, confiscate the loot to return to their sovereigns, and because of the social-distancing directive that extend to mitigating the number of inmates in jails, let the thieves loose on personal recognizance like an efficient open-air courtroom, even when the homeless criminal had multiple warrants for their arrest.

I experienced this exact scenario a handful of times during the first year of the lockdown, which coincided with my final year on the streets. That's why, unlike the last chapter, this chapter has not included headings for arrests.

Until now.

BAIL JUMPING | FELONY | KITSAP COUNTY SUPERIOR COURT

The handle of a large screwdriver protruded from the ignition lock of the early-2000s truck that a guy with tattoos covering every inch of his face and neck was driving south on I-5, a few miles from Centralia. The *piece de resistance* of his tattoo ensemble was a stylized "fuck you" that covered his entire forehead. FU-Guy had stolen the truck while he was on a jaunt in Seattle—he had targeted that exact year, make, and model because he knew the ease with which a hefty screwdriver could be leveraged to bypass the low-tech ignition lock to start such a truck and steal it.

FU-Guy was fresh out of prison, lived in Portland with a female pen pal to whom he had been committedly writing while locked up, and was ready to head back south after having been awake for over a week on a meth run.

"You guys wanna drive to Portland with me?" FU-Guy asked me and another hanger-on when we met him on the Highway the night before.

FU-Guy and his truck had been parked in a little lot in front of a pizza place on 272nd Street. The building was near a popular bus stop for homeless people to run into each other, and behind the building was an equally popular alleyway to smoke, snort, and shoot. FU-Guy had called over the woman who Hanger-On and I had just finished getting high with, asking if she needed anything in the way of drugs. We all ended up in FU-Guy's truck for the rest of the night, as he fed us drugs—the best strategy for a new guy in town to purchase an instant crew amongst the criminal addicts who roamed the streets at night.

When dawn came, FU-Guy proposed that we accompany him on his trip south. The woman left because she had more options than Hanger-on and I did. Leaving town was always an uncomfortable notion—regardless of my lack of stable housing, the familiar environs of the Highway provided a certain sense of security. But I wasn't sure whether I could construct a more profitable alternative for the day ahead.

"We can rob a bank on the way. I'll do the work. One of you just has to drive." FU-Guy strengthened his pitch.

Deal.

I had never robbed a bank before. And I needed the money. So, if FU-Guy were going to do the deed and he merely required emotional-support accomplices, then I'd be the getaway driver of his stolen truck any day.

"One of you guys needs to boost this one type of high-end makeup foundation. It'll cover up my face tattoos and work like the best mask ever.

We gotta wear face masks anyway. But my tattoos are a total giveaway. So, I need this makeup." The torpor of having been awake for days on end lifted as FU-Guy excitedly explained his plan.

Hanger-on and I became FU-Guys' henchmen for the day.

On the drive to Portland, a state trooper appeared to be tailing us for miles after we passed Centralia. We were ever so close to the Columbia River, with Oregon on the other side and Portland a few miles away. But FU-Guy was sweating it, figuratively and literally—beads running down his tattooed bald head and face. If the state trooper had pulled us over, it would have been back to prison for him. Fortunately, the state trooper pulled over at the last rest area before the state line. Everyone in the cab exhaled an audible sigh of relief.

When we arrived in Portland, FU-Guy was physically and emotionally spent. Whatever energy he had left in his tank had been used up focusing on the road, which he said looked like two lanes while that state trooper had been tailing us. FU-Guy told me and Hanger-on that he needed to see his lady before doing anything else—she had been calling him every half hour during the ride down to Portland, and then every few minutes while the state trooper was in sight.

Hanger-on and I suggested that FU-Guy drop us off at the closest home improvement center so we could boost a few goods, and then pick us up later to help us monetize the loot for drugs before robbing a bank of his choice. However, once we got out of FU-Guy's stolen truck, I knew he was going to fall into the comfort of the type of unhealthily indulgent coziness that only a prison pen pal could create, one that had become so suffocatingly permissive that he had been compelled to quit it for a nearly two-week binge in Seattle, but one to which he now felt obliged to crawl back, like a boy who had run away and needed his mommy, into whose lenient softness he would exhaustingly fall out.

Hanger-on and I ended up losing each other. We had entered the supercenter near Providence Park together to get something to eat, agreeing to regroup near the stadium where the Portland Timbers play soccer and strategize how to get back to Seattle. But Hanger-on never showed up.

As night fell, the scene in downtown Portland during the height of the COVID lockdown, just like downtown Seattle, seemed straight out of a zombie apocalypse. There is a particular and peculiar way that junkies who are immersed in their recent dope hit, or tweakers amid a week-long binge, stand in place—legs spread apart wider than shoulder width, back hunched, head slumped, arms hanging in front of them in the same position but slightly lower than a Tyrannosaurus Rex—that makes high junkies and twacked-out tweakers appear like zombies. Place two or three of these typical street folks on street corners abandoned by the lockdown, then add the ever-present evening fog of a Northwest city rolling into the scene, and it's hard to differentiate from a zombie movie.

I spent a cold summer night without drugs amongst the Portland zombies. I didn't have any money or anything to trade, so it felt useless to try making useful friends with any of the street people. FU-Guy had been feeding us meth the entire trip to Portland, so although I wasn't jacked-up, I had enough meth coursing through me, coupled with the nervous energy of being a stranger in a strange land, to compel me to strategize what I'd do the next day.

I implemented my strategy the next day, hitting up my favorite high-end discount fashion store first, as abandoned by customers as every other store I would hit around downtown Portland, all of which were understaffed. I picked a new outfit for myself, as well as two or three of the same items in different sizes, ensuring I was in blind areas behind shelves that shielded me from the security cameras. I stuffed what I wanted into my empty duffel bag, which I had procured in the store.

When I got hungry enough to switch gears and steal food from a grocery store, I was sporting a clean new outfit and a bag of wares for trading. An immense fatigue descended upon me, exacerbated by the extra effort required to navigate a strange land. I got on the bus to the airport, paying my fare just as I'd been doing in Seattle, saying politely that I was homeless and had no money. I figured I could camp out at PDX Airport for a little while to regain energy, assuming it would be as deserted as SeaTac.

It didn't take long for my arrest record to include PDX.

A hand lightly tapping my shoulder and a deep male voice woke me. I had fallen out in front of a window behind a row of chairs. The Port of Portland police officer asked for my ID. I told him I had lost it months ago, so he informed me that he was required to arrest anyone in the airport without an ID. He asked for my name, and I gave him my true identity—I was too tired to think. When he checked my record, he quipped that he would have had to arrest me even if I had been able to produce identification because I was a fugitive from justice, with warrants in another state.

The Port of Portland police officer took my backpack and prized duffel bag, informing me that the Portland jail didn't have room to store them, so the Port of Portland would do so. I could pick up my possessions after being released or pay to have them shipped to me. Although I had stumbled into my way back home, by way of extradition, there went all my loot.

I spent nearly two weeks in the Portland jail, eating and sleeping, electing to stay in my cell during the allotted hours with the general population. I was eventually transported back to the Kitsap County jail, whereupon I was released the day after arriving—the COVID social-distancing rules limited the size of the jail population, so only inmates charged with criminal violence were detained.

* * *

Before Harry and I stumbled upon each other at the Tukwila light rail station, we hadn't seen each other for well over a month. Harry, like the homeless folk with whom he toured, didn't have a phone most of the time. His reason was that he didn't want anyone, mainly the Feds, to have the ability to track him. I, like all the other homeless folks, had my phone stolen regularly, usually when I'd fall asleep on the bus with it in my hand or my backpack in the seat next to me—when the undulations of a moving bus would lull me to sleep after having been awake for days, the sleight of hand that teenage gang members employ to swipe the meager possessions of unsuspecting, fallen-out homeless people is undetectable.

I was mad at Harry for having sent Ronin and his henchman looking for me a few weeks back. Every time he and I would lose touch, he always assumed that I was ditching him. After his goons roughed me up a bit and took my backpack, which contained some nice items that I had been saving specifically for us to trade with his brother-in-law, I had been actively avoiding him. But when we ran into each other at the Tukwila light rail station, he had some meth on him, which he offered, so we were good.

However, Ronin was also with Harry—he and I weren't good. Ronin didn't stick around long, maybe because I wouldn't acknowledge his presence, nor would I acknowledge him henceforth anytime I saw him on the streets, even though he and I used to run together, which had always ended with both of us getting fed up with one another. I'd walk out, just like that, wherever we might be and whatever scheme we may have been plotting.

I wouldn't talk with Ronin until I got off the streets and into recovery.

Over the next few days, Harry and I bought, sold, and traded more profitably than usual, keeping us high and with enough left over to pay for a room for a few days on the Highway. Harry planned to find a couple of the street-walking prostitutes who still paid him dues, let them clean themselves up in the shower, and have our way with them. But we couldn't find his loyal stable of hookers anywhere. Heading back to the room on our last night, we ran into a guy who Harry said didn't like him, but that he had to talk with this guy in private.

The next day, Harry wasn't acting like himself—his signature understated vigor and bravado were missing. I put it down to a weak batch of meth.

That night, we walked up a hill toward the Riverton Park United Methodist Church, where we met a guy who owed Harry. During the COVID lockdown, no one was allowed to congregate, so churches were mostly useless. This church made itself useful by allowing homeless people to set up camp on their grounds. The guy who owed Harry lived in his van. Harry was ambling several paces behind me, and I couldn't stand it any longer.

"What's wrong with you, man?" I turned around and stopped, exasperated.

"I've been shot."

"When? Who? Why didn't you say anything?" I probably should have been sympathetic, but I was pissed off.

"That guy, when you went back to the room. I just push through these things."

I gathered the requisite sympathy (not quite empathy because I've never been shot) to carry the duffel bag that he had been uncomfortably lugging. I took it up the steep hill for him, walking the rest of the way at his pace. When we finally arrived at the van, I put Harry in it.

"How about you rest up here and I'll go sell this bag?"

By bag, I didn't mean a bag of drugs. I meant the exceptional knock-off of a designer bag that Harry had found hanging from a wrought-iron handrail while we were walking around Renton. It was the weirdest thing for someone to leave just hanging there—maybe the previous owner was hoping to serendipitously gift it to an unsuspecting young girl, who would have been astounded by her luck.

Instead, an old, formerly incarcerated homeless tourist snapped it up. I took one look at the tag inside and knew it was just an excellent fake. The brand name was stitched on ever so slightly crooked, but that was the only thing wrong with it. Harry had been adamant that it was authentic, and no one could tell him differently. We had been trying to sell it for days—only cartel dudes were interested, and they didn't offer more than

$100. Harry maintained its authenticity, so we continued to decline all offers until now.

"Yeah. Get a $100 from a cartel dude, or maybe that much in black, and we can trade with my brother-in-law in the morning." Harry's speech was labored.

"I'll be back in a few hours," I guaranteed.

Plans fall apart. I did manage to find a cartel dude at a motel halfway between Tukwila and Federal Way to take the nigh perfectly constructed fake designer bag, but it was a trade for heroin and meth. I ended up snorting a line while sitting at a bus stop. A cute junkie flirted with me. When she got on the bus and I stayed, I couldn't find the bag of heroin. I snorted the rest of the meth to console myself.

I didn't want to go back to Harry empty-handed, as he always got on me for tricking out drugs for girls. I spent the next day looking for ways to replace the dope. Nothing.

Harry was gone when I returned to the van late in the middle of the night.

In about three weeks, I would be picked up by the police for shoplifting at the Renton Landing Target store. The police car would roll up to the bus stop shelter, where I anxiously awaited, carrying a tent, two winter coats, a sleeping bag, and two pairs of active noise-canceling earbuds. The weather had turned cold, and although I habitually eschewed preparing for cold weather the entire time I was on the streets—viewing such preparations as an existential admission to being stuck in a hopelessly homeless predicament—the thought of another winter having nowhere to lay my head and bundle up when no other options existed was downright miserable. The policeman would seem uninterested, just another low-level retail crime he was forced to process, but then he would run my name and see that I had a cocktail of felony and misdemeanor warrants. He would confiscate the stolen items and return them to Target.

The policeman would take me to that creepy SCORE jail, from which I would be extradited to Kitsap County, as it had superior-court jurisdiction over me. I would spend Halloween, Thanksgiving, and Christmas in the Kitsap County Jail.

Every time I've gone to jail, it seems that a book has been waiting there. This time in Port Orchard, Dr. Gabor Maté's *In the Realm of Hungry Ghosts* was that book. This tome turned the addiction treatment landscape on its head by convincingly arguing that substance use disorders are less a disease and more a result of early childhood trauma, continuing into adulthood through self-inflicted traumatic events during active addiction. In one passage, the good doctor posits that "One characteristic of personality disorder, a condition with which substance abusers are very commonly diagnosed, is a kind of flip-flopping between idealization of another person and intense dislike, even hatred. There is no middle ground, where both the positive and negative qualities are acknowledged and accepted."

I shuddered in recognition. When anyone (family, friends, and even therapists) would warn me about the toxicity of whichever relationship I might be in at the time—my ex-wife, Diana, Kaylee, Ava—I would drop the concerned party, cutting them off completely. After having finally liberated myself from a trauma bond, I'd become overwhelmed with hatred for my erstwhile trauma-bond partners. I usually attribute that phenomenon to having genuinely loved that person, as many sages have said that only true love can turn into certifiable hatred.

The same goes with business partners. Harry was right—during the weeks that we couldn't find each other on the streets, I was glad that he wasn't around. He was controlling and made me a subordinate, always nit-picking at this and that about my behavior or appearance (though I could understand that last part when the sores on my face became so noticeable that I resorted to covering them up with makeup foundation matching my skin color, which I would steal from the makeup aisle during boosting excursions).

The image of Harry cooped up in a dirty van with a gunshot wound made me feel like I had abandoned him for a little bit of flirting with a cute junkie who stole our loot.

Everything Harry said about me was true. I was an awful friend.

PART II

RECOVERY

Chapter 7

Phase I

Where does recovery start?

It was easier to pinpoint where my descent began—with my first taste of methamphetamine and the unparalleled amount of dopamine that it dumped into my brain. Though it would be just as accurate to say that my descent began with my first taste of alcohol, marijuana, cocaine, or ecstasy. But that can be a trite notion, just as I could say my path to enlightenment began when I descended into the life of a full-time criminal on the streets. But recovery? Where to begin?

If I use my current favorite analogy of how the Tlaxcala chose and trained their community leaders—subjecting arrogant and ambitious would-be leaders to public humiliation, isolation, blood-letting, fasting, sleep deprivation, and finally to a regimen of strict moral training—then I can say that recovery began when I became a participant in the strict moral training program that started it all for me: Kitsap County Drug Court.

I was stipulated into the Drug Court program on January 28, 2021. The path to that day began when I was picked up by the police for the last time, extradited from the SCORE jail, still wearing my jail stripes, to the Kitsap County Jail, where the booking photo shown in the Introduction was taken. I dried out for a couple of days before appearing in court. Before it was my turn to appear in front of the judge, he told the guy before me that, since it was his first time being arrested and jailed, he would be PR'd. That's how things went during the COVID era, and that's what I expected would happen to me. If anything other than that happened, I would be appalled.

"Now, Mr. Leyva is another story," the judge proclaimed before I could take a seat at the table next to my public defender. "Mr. Leyva has a history of jumping bail and skipping court appearances. So, I won't give him another chance to behave in such a manner. Bail is set at $150,000."

I couldn't believe what I was hearing. The judge wouldn't even listen to the arguments in my defense. I looked at my public defender. He just shrugged his shoulders and lightly patted my shoulder as some form of unsatisfactory encouragement.

I was taken back to my cell. I fumed for hours. How could they hold me in this COVID-infested tank? There must be some directive against this. I wasn't a violent offender—just a thief, no harm to anyone other than the corrupt capitalist system. When it was my section's turn for free time, I stood in line at the pay phones, my public defender's card in hand, and shot daggers at the other inmates calling their babies' mothers and talking forever about nothing important. When it was finally my turn, I called my public defender, knowing full well that his office would be closed, and proceeded to leave an invective-filled rant about the unacceptable circumstances in which his failed service had left me.

Luckily, this half Asian dude started a conversation while we glanced at the television. In jail, similar races stick together—whites with whites, blacks with blacks, Asians and Natives with themselves—especially when sitting down for meals. Growing up in a predominantly white suburb, I have always tended to hang with white people. I'm most comfortable as the only dark token in groups. But I wasn't about to break jail rules.

"You want some clear?" Half Asian asked in a covert volume.

"You got some?"

"Yeah. One of the Sureños brought in some butt drugs. My girl puts money on his books so he can get commissary when we get moved to general population."

During COVID, inmates were placed in isolation upon first entering, which meant single cells in a pod section. After two weeks in quarantine, we were then moved to general population, which meant dormitories with multiple bunk beds and access to a menu of food and accessories that could be purchased with credit through someone on the outside putting money into your account.

"I don't have anything to give you."

"It's cool, man. I got you." A minute later, Half Asian returned from his cell with a book in which he had placed a couple of nice-sized nuggets wrapped in a tiny envelope made from a torn corner of a piece of paper.

Half Asian had just bought himself an ally.

It took a few days for my public defender to arrive and meet with me. The corrections officer (CO) called my name and led me to a meeting room. The county lawyer waiting in the room was not the person who sat with me in front of the judge.

"My name is Justin, and I'll be your public defender going forward. Before we start, I want to make clear that I heard your message, and I take umbrage at some of the things you said about the public defender who represented you in court. He is one of the top attorneys in the county."

"Yeah. Maybe my soliloquy was a little out of line. Actually, it was more of a diatribe." I tried to apologize.

"This is the first time I've heard an inmate use the word 'soliloquy'…and then correct himself with more accuracy."

"I was an English major, and I used to write proposals to get corporate resources for projects and venture capital for startups."

After a pause to process what he had just heard, Justin continued, "Be that as it may, you know you're facing prison."

"Let's take it to trial." I thought the COVID restrictions limiting the number of inmates per square foot would save the day. Up to that point,

I had avoided paying the consequences for my actions, so I expected something to break my way again.

"I don't see how that will help. There are photos of you taking a man's backpack whose identity you stole. And in the Walmart where you tried using another person's credit card. You were apprehended in the car that you stole. You were extradited from Portland as a fugitive from justice. The list goes on."

"Isn't there anything you can do?" I felt the actual weight of the consequences.

"A plea might be your best alternative. It would decrease the time you'd serve." This was Justin's best shot, and it sucked.

"I was high the whole time." My confession didn't have a specific intention. I was merely providing color commentary to my actions.

"Hmm. Have you heard of Drug Court?" Justin arched an eyebrow, "Minimum 18-month program. It's divided into four phases. You serve your time in the community under strict judicial supervision. However, you must appear in court every week. You're required to attend outpatient addiction treatment classes and submit to random urinalysis to make sure you're off drugs. Phase 1 lasts three months, Phase 2 lasts four months, Phase 3 lasts five months, and Phase 4 lasts six months. Those are minimums. Most people mess up, so they tack on more time depending on the phase. If and when you do make a mistake, it's best to be honest about it and come clean. They'll usually show leniency under those circumstances. It's a strict program. You have to sign away any rights to privacy. But not only would you avoid prison, all your felony charges would be dismissed."

"Can I see the application?" I asked sheepishly. Justin fished the document from his briefcase. The main part required an essay. "I got this, man, I'm a writer by trade."

"Well, if you want to be the A+ student."

I spent the next few days barely talking with any of the inmates, including Half-Asian. He was so perturbed by my keeping my head down in pen and paper that he kept asking what I was doing, and then sarcastically answering himself that I was naturally tweaking. And I was tweaking on two documents: the Drug Court application and my master plan to leverage the newfound legitimacy that the dismissal of felony charges would afford.

Like a good product manager, I created a roadmap (because plans fall apart, but roadmaps provide a destination and milestones that allow for course corrections when the unexpected, expectedly, happen), and a pitch deck—a business plan in the form of a PowerPoint presentation—but as I was in jail without access to Microsoft Office, I did it all by hand. I was definitely tweaking. I kept the master plan—I'm looking at it right now as I type, trying to discern what I meant, laughing at my former self's inappropriate swagger and misplaced drive. It's a well-designed document, in a Unabomber way—I labored over the layout, and as a nefarious business plan, it was well thought out.

Professional Drug Addict

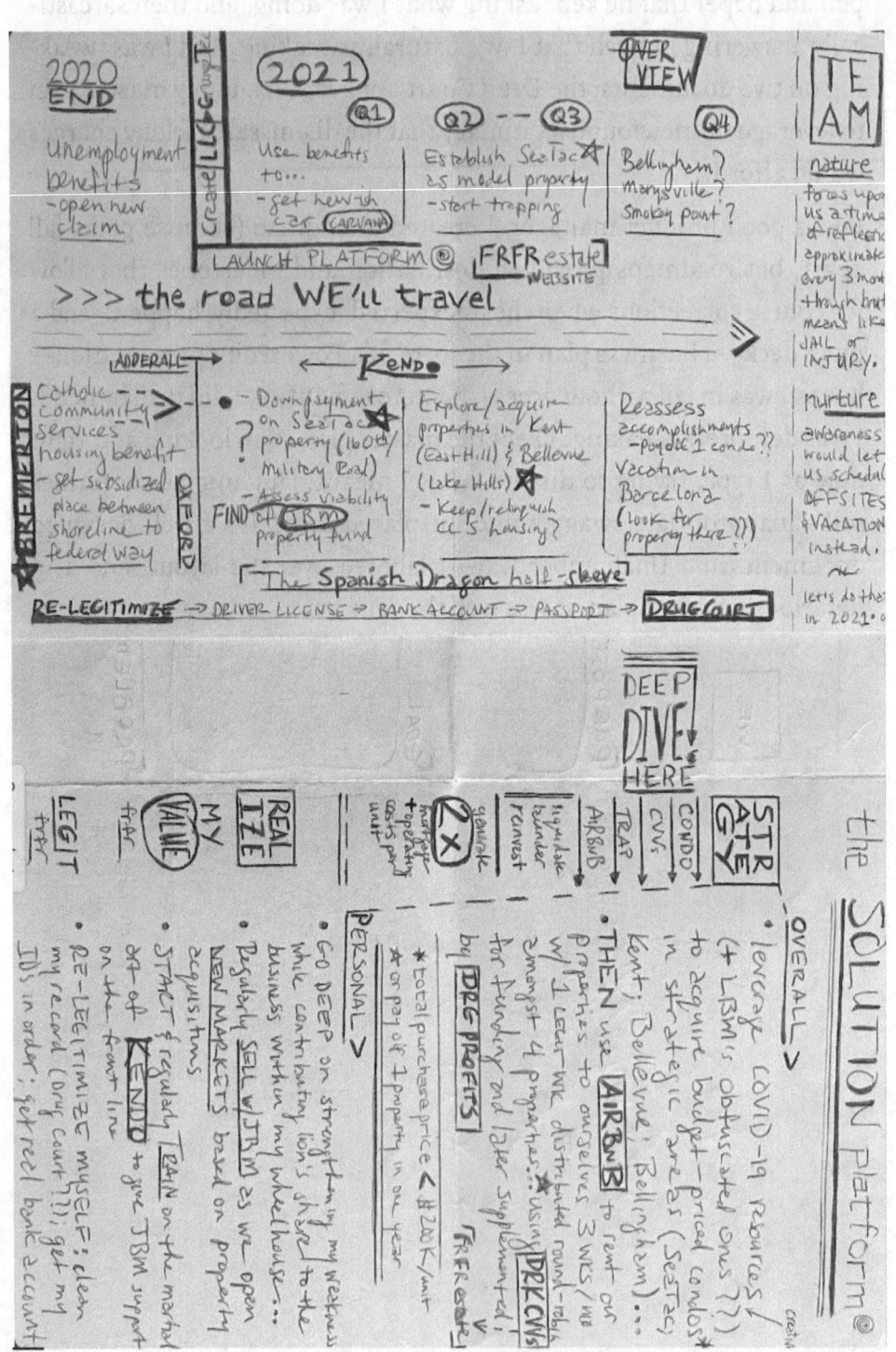

The idea originated from my time spent with a brother and sister duo who lived in an Airbnb condo in SeaTac, just a few blocks east of the airport. Harry's nephew introduced us—he found me tired and forlorn, sitting in the bus shelter across from the Washington Memorial Park cemetery. It was during the three weeks between Harry's disappearance after getting shot and the police picking me up for the last time. I told Harry's nephew how I'd let him down, couldn't find him anywhere, and since then, had lost the confidence to boost.

Harry's nephew took me under his wing and brought me to meet the SeaTac brother and sister. We immediately hit it off—they had a middle-class upbringing in Renton; the brother had been a logger who had almost been killed in a logging accident; the sister had worked for Nordstrom and had that blonde Nordstrom look about her; they appreciated my polite manners, which were hard to come by on the streets; the sister's baby daddy had started doing well for himself, getting in with an operation that bought any and every catalytic converter that he could steal, so he was paying her rent on a two-bedroom Airbnb condo.

The Renton siblings harbored street people whom they found agreeable and useful. They liked me better than Harry's nephew, telling me so when he was out and about. Harry's nephew could feel it and would put me down whenever he was around. I accepted the treatment because, well, he was Harry's nephew, and Harry was my partner.

When I couldn't stand the put-downs and microaggressions any longer, I left the Airbnb to commit the fateful act that would land me in the Kitsap County Jail, where I devised a diabolical plan revolving around Airbnb condos and dark CVVs...

1. COVID UNEMPLOYMENT INSURANCE: Leverage COVID resources creatively to acquire budget-priced condos in strategic areas, with SeaTac as the hub. I had been diligently submitting unemployment claims since near the beginning of the COVID lockdown, when a woman standing at the steps of the Tukwila Transit Center entrance was telling passersby that the government was providing everyone with unemployment payments to weather the tough economic times. I had not been able to collect unemployment insurance since leaving my last job under a cloud, but this news gave me hope. However, I never managed to get through the massive number of calls the unemployment call center had to field—the call of drugs echoing throughout the day, every day, supplanted any ounce of the patience required to navigate the call queue. Hence, the diabolical roadmap began with finding a way to finally reach the unemployment office and identifying the exact tasks needed to overcome the obstacles to my startup funds.

2. AIRBNB PROPERTY: Then, I thought that I could somehow leverage the overflowing COVID money to buy a condominium (completely unaware that the enforcement of work-from-home policies had driven real estate prices through the roof). The strategy included listing the property on Airbnb, but not entirely for legitimate purposes.

3. LIQUIDATE DARK CVVs THROUGH THE AIRBNB PROPERTY: The property would function as a liquidation platform for ill-gotten credit cards. The last time Aiden and I worked together, he showed me how to purchase credit card information on the dark web, but he never had a way to cash out the credit limits. In my dark plan, I would rent the property for three weeks using dark credit cards, the proceeds of which would be funneled into my Airbnb account. We would allow the property to be booked by a valid Airbnb user one week per month, to maintain its legitimacy. During the three weeks of dark-CVV liquidation, the strategy included Harry leveraging his connections to trap the place out, generating a diversified income through drug sales.

4. REVOLVING ACQUISITION FUND: The money generated through diversified channels would create a fund, allowing us to purchase more properties—in Kent, Tukwila, Aurora, hell, even Bellevue—that would become a portfolio of dark-CVV liquidators and drug hubs, with me as the squeaky-clean front thanks to Drug Court.

I had it all figured out.

I spent the next month biding my time in jail, trading my tray of biscuits and gravy (I don't know why the criminal population loves that dish so much) for Seroquel pills so that I could sleep throughout the day to avoid the reality of jail life, reading the books that had been waiting for me, and getting accepted into Drug Court.

"Is there any way for me to get PR'd before my Drug Court stipulation? That's almost two months away," I complained to Justin when he came to visit.

"The only place that the judge will release you to is an Oxford House."

Ugh. I wanted nothing to do with Oxford Houses. They just seemed so… abstinent.

But needs must, so I set up interviews. Everyone kept telling me how difficult it was to get accepted, so I prepared as if it were a job interview, asking other inmates who had lived in Oxford Houses about the usual array of questions and what the answers might be. I nailed my first interview.

I was PR'd on December 30, 2020. I headed to the Hewitt Oxford House in West Bremerton, but on my way, I took a detour to Issaquah to pick up some money from my father. He was just happy that I was out of jail and seemingly, finally, on my ascent.

I arrived at the Hewitt Oxford House around 10:30 p.m., soaked from the rain. I was put in the reentry bed—reserved for new tenants coming straight from jail or intensive inpatient treatment—at the top of the stairs in a little cubby in the hallway. I was glad to have a place to rest my head.

But what a depressing place.

* * *

Just over two weeks into my Oxford House sojourn, I was utterly, decidedly, unmitigatedly broke.

Jeremy, a young fellow Drug Court participant, had a small COVID unemployment claim, so he let me use his government-issued debit card to buy myself a pack of cigarettes at the corner store a few blocks down the street. I will never forget that act of kindness. He didn't know me at all. I could have run up a tab. But even though he knew where I lived and could try to collect if I had given in to my triggers when he had handed over his debit card, his gesture epitomizes the camaraderie and honor amongst desperately recovering thieves nurtured and sown in recovery residences. That's how it's supposed to work. I still run into Jeremy at 12-Step meetings around town, and he remains one of my favorite people in recovery.

The Oxford House model works when senior tenants lead house operations by taking junior tenants under their wing. The model falls apart when senior tenants become less engaged with household matters as their lives become more stable and fruitful, pulling their attention toward the next step in their life progression, which leaves junior tenants to fend for themselves. This is the knock on the Oxford House model—criminal drug addicts fresh out of prison, jail, and intensive inpatient treatment programs do not possess the coping skills and resiliency required for self-governance, leaving them prone to relapse, which leads to expulsion from the Oxford House, which leads to homelessness, which leads to continued drug use and recidivism.

Another Oxford housemate, who shall remain unnamed, got me a gram of meth that kept me high for almost two weeks. I knew that I'd stipulate into Drug Court near the end of January, and I wanted to get high right up to the week before, as I'd heard that they would require a urinalysis. I couldn't believe that tiny bit of meth would go so far. The loss of tolerance had turned me into a cheap date.

Every night for two weeks, I'd curl up in my reentry bed in the hallway, frantically looking for ways to implement my dastardly plan on the laptop that I had traded this young Samoan gangster on the Highway for a quarter ounce of meth. It was the one item that I had saved from my street days generating the highest return on investment.

During the day, I would engage in minor revenue-generating activities to accomplish the second-most important tactic of my desperate strategy: buy dark CVVs.

I downloaded the Tor browser and searched "buy credit card information."

The Tor Project is a nonprofit organization that developed an "onion routing" mechanism to create internet connections that conceal who is talking to whom. The creators, who worked at the U.S. Naval Research Lab, developed a way to route traffic through multiple servers, encrypting it at each step. It's a noble cause that has become the gateway to the dark web.

I quickly found a long and detailed listing, containing everything I was looking for. When I noticed that the service provider included their Telegram handle (the most notoriously private and secure messaging app—the platform's data centers are spread across a complex corporate structure of shell companies in various jurisdictions to avoid compliance with government subpoenas to protect the data not covered by end-to-end encryption), my mind was made up.

I followed the service provider's instructions, sending $45 through Western Union. The Western Union teller warned me of the fraud flag on the service provider's address in Vietnam, but that news made them even more credible. Of course it's fraudulent. That's what this person is all about, and they were located in Southeast Asia, where they know a thing or two about scams. I urged the teller to send the money.

I never heard back from the Vietnamese scammer. Touché.

As much as I admired the design of the Vietnamese scam, playing on the desperation of would-be dark webbers, I was left completely broke again and even more desperate. Furthermore, the recovery weight I put on from all the junk food that my food stamps gave me the purchasing power to acquire and gorge on, trying desperately to fill the unfillable internal void that drugs used to mask for an ephemeral moment, made me even more sluggish. Being out of drugs and careful of the looming

Drug Court stipulation, I also had no meth inspiration to turn to—I was a broke sloth.

I had a copy of my old driver's license in my Outlook email from years ago, which I used to make replicas of my license numerous times on the streets (some places accepted it as a valid ID). I uploaded it to the unemployment insurance site as my first form of ID, but I still had to produce a second form. Without a valid license, I couldn't get a replacement Social Security card, which would serve as my second form of ID.

Tens of thousands of dollars of backpay from a year of submitting claims were dammed up, just waiting to be released. If only Google weren't so stupid and believed that I was me, and not the person who hacked into my Gmail account—I'm pretty sure this happened the last time my phone was stolen while I was asleep on the bus, with my phone unlocked—then I could access 17 years' worth of documents. I signed up for Gmail when giving away 1GB was a massive deal. My Gmail contained copies of my Social Security card and passport, but whoever hacked into my account was surely disappointed—an identity-theft treasure trove rendered worthless by a homeless credit score.

As I mindlessly munched on late-night potato chips, soda, and pastries, I mindfully scrolled through my Outlook, the only historical email account to which I had access, hoping beyond hope that somewhere in the unending cache of emails was something that might produce a second piece of identification. The date stamps were approaching five years old, my eyesight was getting blurry, and the food crumbs on the bed made me itch.

Then, I saw a subject line that read "PP." I opened the email and saw that the body of the message was empty; there was only an attachment. I double-clicked it, and lo and behold: a copy of my passport.

The next day, I got up early and called the unemployment office. I got through right away, which felt like hitting a jackpot. I asked if I could upload the recently discovered copy of my passport—would that work?

Yes.

It took another week to find out they needed proof that I was in dire straits because of COVID. Easy and simple—I uploaded a letter from the Oxford House housing coordinator, stating that I would be kicked out in three weeks unless I paid that month's rent (this letter is de rigueur for anyone applying for rental assistance from a community agency), along with a free credit report, showing my house had been foreclosed during the COVID lockdown.

I called back a few days later and received news that, because I had diligently submitted unemployment claims all of last year, I would receive one year's worth of back pay ($43,000) and continuing weekly unemployment payments (over $1000) based on my old tech salary.

I felt like a rock star again.

* * *

"Wait. You got $50,000 deposited in your bank account in one day?" Laurel, my Drug Court compliance specialist (part case manager, part compliance officer), gasped. Not exactly what happened, but close enough and sounded much cooler than the precise truth. I wanted to impress Laurel—she was young and pretty, with a massive heart but firm boundaries for someone her age. There was a significant age gap between us, and as she exuded a spirit of a genuine do-gooder who had consciously drawn lines that she wouldn't allow others to cross, I felt like the absent parent who had forced her into a parentalized role. I decided to view her as a much younger sister who had her shit together, tasked with straightening out all the black sheep on her caseload. "Is it a trigger?" Laurel continued her line of questioning.

"Um…I don't think so." That answer was a bunch of shit—within a short pause, I calculated that affirming her question might cause Drug Court to place limitations on what I could do with the money, and I wanted no part of any limitations. This money was mine. I waited a year for it and put in hard work and effort.

Not sure if Laurel believed me—all I know is, from that day forward, an image of Laurel as a little angel on my shoulder appeared, asking "Is it a trigger?" every time I wanted to do something with the money that Drug Court forbade. Of course, it was a trigger—all I wanted to do was go on the run, get the fanciest motel room around (not a hotel, as I wanted the money to go further), buy a literal pound of meth, hit up my bevy of prostitutes (and find new ones online), walk the Highway, track down Harry, run into other folks, bring everyone back to my room, and party until the money ran it, which it wouldn't for however long the government continued to pay people off for having (accidentally) unleashed a virus that a conglomerate of governments had created.

But I didn't run. I was playing the long game.

No, I wasn't trying to turn a new leaf. I needed Drug Court to clean my record so that I would once again be a valuable front for the operation I had hatched in jail. Now, it was time to track down Harry. I wanted to give him some of this money, since I'd abandoned him, shot, in a crumby old van, as well as tell him about my vision of a dark CVV-financed and drug money-operated Highway property portfolio. I remembered that I had one of the phone numbers of one of the cartel guys who regularly fielded calls for Harry. I thumbed through my call log and found one I didn't recognize with a 253-area code. That must be it.

I sent an experimental text...

ME: "I'm looking for Harry. Please tell him it's Arnel. I got picked up last November. I'm in drug court in Bremerton. I have money for him."

In the meantime, I spent my money in a way that served as a replacement for my old life, but that kept me safe from The Life, while making me feel like a do-gooder. Every night, as midnight approached, I would walk the streets. I missed the chthonian energy of the streets, an ambiguous freedom that I had never felt before becoming homeless, and one in which I no longer had the liberty to participate. I kept a stack of 10 x $100 bills in the back-cover folder of my Moleskine notebook. I would take a couple of bills with me on my walks, and whenever I ran into street people, I would hand them a $100 bill. I wouldn't wait for a reaction, wouldn't ask for anything (in my old life, I'd expect a specific quantity of drugs) in return. These transactions gave me such a high.

After the final such transaction (once I'd looked at my bank account and seen how quickly it had dwindled), I cried. I remembered what Carol, my first Drug Court counselor, had said to me during our most recent conversation—with crystal clarity, I told her of the three distinct times that people on the streets, completely out-of-their-faces high, said that I would start a revolution: once while keeping a fire going with hand sanitizer and rubbing alcohol in the dumpster area behind the Des Moines Safeway during the middle of my first winter on the Highway; another at the end of that same winter, waiting for the all-night bus at the Sea-Tac Airport Transit Station; and finally, waiting at the bus stop in front of Bartell Drugs during my last long, hot, climate-change summer on the streets, shielding a couple cronies from prying eyes as they administered their daily dose.

"I think you will start a revolution…and it will have something to do with homelessness," Carol assured me.

As a member of my surrogate Drug Court family, Carol would play the slightly off-kilter sage, as most sages are wont, like a grand-aunt whose debaucherous life molded her into a trustworthy and accurate seer. That's the role she would play during my 27 months in Drug Court, planting seeds in my mind that would blossom.

It took a few days before Harry texted back.

HARRY'S EMISSARY: "This is from Harry- 'Why you always dipping on me?'"

ME: "I didn't dip. I lost part of the stuff and and tried to boost some things to sell. I didn't want to come back empty-handed. You were gone when I returned. I'm only doing drug court so I can clean my record and become valuable again. I finally got my unemployment. I can western-union 2 grand to you or meet you somewhere. Lmk."

To sway Harry, I attached a screenshot of my bank balance, showing tens of thousands of dollars.

The next day, I received another message from his messenger…

HARRY'S EMISSARY: "Looks like a setup."

Wtf? Know what? Screw you, bro. You think you're all that. You think Drug Court has me cooperating with the Feds to reel you in. Nah, man. This ain't about you. Drug Court doesn't give a shit about you. They care about me.

My final interaction with Harry gave me a new affinity for Drug Court.

Waking up to this textual commotion threw me off-balance, so to calm myself down, I decided to double up and snort two Wellbutrin pills. In jail, I had heard of the stimulating effect of crushed Wellbutrin up the nose, though I never found anyone who would trade theirs with me. Once I got out, settled into my surroundings, and stopped doing meth, the first item on my task list was go to the community health services, and tell the physician about my stimulant use disorder.

Just as opioid addiction is treated with Suboxone or methadone during the early stages to counteract cravings, which, if left untreated, create a direct route to relapse, Wellbutrin is used in much the same way for stimulant users. It is, however, a weak substitute. I was hoping for Adderall, but as that is an honest-to-goodness amphetamine, it is on Drug Court's banned substance list. Shoving Wellbutrin up your nose is a pretty good alternative.

I developed a ritual…

1. Soak the Wellbutrin pill in hot water for a few seconds, causing the plastic coating to slide off with a gentle twist of the forefinger and thumb.
2. Let the pill dry for a few minutes.
3. Place the pill on a China dinner plate, cover it with a pliable plastic sheet (I made one using a long piece of packing tape folded over to create two slippery sides), and use just enough force to crush the pill without having bits fly out from under the cover.
4. Use a credit card to cut the crushed nuggets into a fine powder and then into thick parallel lines on the fine China.
5. Finally, after the mindfulness of the fine motor movements and anticipation of my ritual created an introductory high…snort

(the powder's bitter remnants creating a lovely drip down my throat reminiscent of bad cocaine).

After snorting the second pill, I received a call from Carol.

"What are you doing?"

"What do you mean?" I could taste the Wellbutrin drip in the back of my throat.

"You've missed your last three UAs. We're here to help you." Carol's voice dropped to a comforting tone.

"What are you talking about? I've called the UA line every day for the past two weeks, and the letter of my last name hasn't been called." I was adamant.

Each participant is assigned to a treatment agency when entering Drug Court. Mine was Kitsap Recovery Center (KRC). Each agency has its own system for administering random urinalysis. KRC's was color-coded—participants were instructed to call the UA line every day and listen for their color to be called, which meant they needed to go to the agency and take a piss test. However, the message also included CPS (Child Protective Services) participants who were required to provide UAs for their cases, and their randomization was based on the first letter of their last names—the UA line message states explicitly that participants should listen to the entire message before hanging up.

But I was a rock star again. I was better than everyone else in Drug Court, including the judge, counselors, compliance specialists, and especially the other participants. Rock stars only listen to the first part of the message—we can't be bothered listening to an entire criminal justice-involved message.

I gave Carol that very explanation (except for the last part about being a rock star again).

"That's rich." She wasn't having it.

Laurel called me not long afterwards. I gave her the same explanation (again, excluding the rock-star bit).

"How do you expect me to believe that? This isn't the best way to start Drug Court, even if it's true. The judge wants you to appear in court today, rather than your normal appearance two days from now. Can I trust you to come in?"

"Yes, of course," I assured her.

Later that day, I stood before Judge H. She would become the archetype for the emotionally stable and available parent I had heard of in my youth, but always doubted existed. Judge H possessed an equanimity that I never witnessed waver. Even when she brought the hammer down on me that day, she was gentle.

"Arnel, you've missed three UAs in a row. In the court's eyes, that's the same as a dirty UA. I've heard that you had some confusion about the instructions on the UA line. We've considered that. However, your behavior of late has concerned us. You were allowed to skip inpatient treatment before you stipped into Drug Court because, unlike many of the participants, you had secured stable housing in a sober environment. But it seems that an inpatient stay would do you good. We're sending you to JOTC (James Oldham Treatment Center). Your bed date isn't for another week and a half, so we're going to put you in jail for safekeeping. I trust you understand."

"Yes, ma'am." I was in no position to argue.

* * *

If my descent into homeless criminalization was one significant slippery slope, then recovery is a long and winding road…that goes through Yakima.

I kept my notebook from JOTC. I'm reading from it as I write this chapter.

I'm no longer ashamed of where I've been, where I came from, what I've been through. Okay, maybe a little, but nothing like before, when I didn't want anyone to know that I was living with nine other men in a rundown Oxford House. But I'm having the same difficulty writing about this subject as I did writing about my ex-wife. Now I know why—this section will include insights into my family.

Last year, after I'd been in real recovery, not just abstinence, for two years, after I'd done what I kept telling anyone who would listen that I would do—launch a social service agency—started to come together as a tangible vision during my stint in JOTC. I was at the annual Kitsap County Drug Court Christmas party, where I ran into Christyn, my Drug Court therapist for two pivotal years. Like Laurel, Christyn was young and pretty. Between the two of them, I was forced to develop a different way of interacting with such women whom, until that point, I had only known as prostitutes and casual encounters. I became intimate with two women who were charged to care for my mental health and well-being, in the process showing me that what I had thought was intimacy was merely a drug-addled surrogate.

Christyn had once said to me that she could see me in the media, and at the party, I told her she was right, as I was writing my memoir with a book deal in hand. Nevertheless, I did not intend to write about my ex-wife or my family; rather, I would focus solely on my time on the streets and my ensuing recovery. Christyn just looked at me with that therapeutic, don't-kid-yourself look of hers.

The best way to describe intensive inpatient programs for addiction treatment to the uninitiated would be to call it "sober camp"—28 days of respite away from the hustle and bustle of The Life; bunking with other justice system-involved drug addicts in close-quartered dormitories; learning about the science of addiction (psychoeducation) and coping skills that neglected and abused children were never taught by caretakers who didn't know better; held to a structured and disciplined schedule to begin the indoctrination of those very habits; allowed (required) to play games in the clear and warm Eastern Washington weather to wear us out like hyper puppies; and, ultimately, build approximately one month of clean and sober time.

I didn't know it when I got there, but my psychoeducation would revolve around codependency. During my last fateful counseling session with

Carol, she intimated that she saw in me a level of codependency rivalling her own, and that it was the foundation of my addiction. I may learn how to manage my addiction to the point that cravings would dissipate, but managing my codependency would be a lifelong daily task.

Just like jail, there was a book waiting for me at JOTC. It wasn't on a bookshelf. One of the counselors gave it to me, like an artifact to offer at an altar: *Codependent No More* by Melody Beattie, the originator of the term and magnum opus of Al-Anon. The book describes the characteristics of people addicted to alcoholics and addicts, unknowingly enabling their partner/child/parent to continue their wretched behavior.

One of the counselors would give a talk about the subject during an all-hands lecture in the auditorium. I couldn't get away from the subject.

My time at JOTC marked the beginning of my understanding of the patterns and characteristics that are woven throughout the previous vignettes in this book. One of the main tasks during my 28-day stay was to keep a journal that would inform the autobiography assignment. I wrote mine in fits and starts from April Fool's Day to Easter...

April Fool's Day 2021

I romanticized my perpetual unhappiness as the archetypal existential angst through which all great literature is created—my version of The Portrait of the Artist as a Catcher in the Rye. I was shit with money to start with anyway. If I overspent to compensate for my perceived lack of material accoutrements and emotional support that I saw the other kids in my Bellevue neighborhood receiving, my parents would be there to catch me. Needing to be bailed out was one of the only situations in which I received the attention and affection I craved.

Codependency...putting someone else's needs above your own to your detriment, in an attempt to control the other's behavior. It's that last part that differentiates it from service. Never understood it until the all-hands lecture on the concept. What a revelation! It liberates me while tripping me TF out. My codependency has driven the destruction that I've left in my wake. I've always downplayed this characteristic in me, and the consequent addictive personality, because I don't remember experiencing the sort of trauma that typically accompanies that diagnosis. Equally, my parents were not substance abusers. So, how could I have become a codependent when the classic environment for producing such behaviors wasn't present?

The all-hands lecture showed me the way. The counselor explained how keeping secrets about a parent's addiction and the turmoil it causes within the family dynamic instills codependent habits in the children. They assume responsibility for perpetuating the environment in which the addict parent can continue to create emergencies that become the family's priorities to the detriment of rearing the children to become well-balanced and responsible adults.

Damn. My five siblings and I were left without parental supervision starting when my oldest sister was around 12 years old, with the rest of us following approximately two years subsequently in age. My parents both worked two jobs, chasing the American dream. They told us kids not to discuss the situation with anyone outside the house. Otherwise, they would get in trouble, and we would be taken away. That's the first memory I can reposition based on my newfound understanding of codependency. It's hard to blame my parents here.

Easter 2021

My parents weren't getting hammered, wasted, or high. They were out making money. Sometimes, they'd stay out late and get together with their Filipino community to let loose. They were just over 30 years old when they started leaving six children at home, so how can I fault them? But now I see how asking us kids to keep their secret, making it our secret, affected me. I always suspected that our lack of coping and life skills as adults (at least mine) stemmed from being left to our own devices—kids can't teach kids about life because we don't know. The question of how I could have inherited the habits of addicts from two non-druggie, hardly drinkers, makes sense now.

What happened to us was not uncommon within the Filipino community. It was common in the Philippines, but it was tied to upward mobility in the U.S. My mother would tell us kids about the son or daughter of other Filipinos, about the things they were achieving in white society while behaving the way good Filipino sons and daughters should—living at home until they married and/ or graduated from university. I always thought she wanted us to be successful in the tra-

ditional sense—to overachieve whenever the opportunity presented itself—so she could one-up or at least keep up with the other immigrant mothers running the same race. Which makes me wonder: Can codependency be an endemic trait at the level of an entire culture or class? Immigrants trying to gain a foothold in their adopted country to prove they belong.

* * *

After my release from JOTC, I was an even bigger (though newly psychoeducated) asshole when I pulled up to my Oxford House.

For all the quiet insight that the intensive inpatient environment afforded, I managed to complete two avaricious tasks that I had started before Drug Court abruptly confiscated me from my nascent rock stardom. I had purchased a 2006 Audi A8 in beautiful condition, even scheduling its delivery from Lake City to my Oxford House in Bremerton, but the transaction had to wait until my release. I rescheduled the pick-up for the day of my release—the Greyhound bus dropped me off in downtown Seattle, a mere 5-minute bus ride from the Highway. As tempting as hitting up street folks and showing off seemed, I had more important business requiring my attention.

I checked the time on my new Tag Heuer Monaco, the other avaricious task that I accomplished. I had ordered the watch before leaving for JOTC; it had been my dream watch ever since I noticed it on the *Breaking Bad* episode in which Jesse gives Walter the very same watch as a birthday gift; I had the delivery address changed to the addiction treatment facility, as I didn't want a $6000 piece of masculine jewelry ending up in the hands of a well-intentioned but not completely trustworthy Oxford housemate.

After picking up the car, I stopped at my favorite high-end discount store to buy (not boost) new threads and sunglasses.

Everyone was surprised when I pulled up to my Oxford House—no one expected me because I hadn't announced my arrival. One of my housemate's girlfriends, all of whom hung around all day and stayed the night as if they lived there (which Oxford House rules forbid, but we didn't care, because we ran that joint now), was sitting on the porch when I climbed the stairs.

"You look like you came from Beverly Hills."

Like I said—a much larger asshole. And that's how I would operate until Drug Court found me out.

I was already into my fourth month of what should have been a three-month phase, which made me feel like a failure. If I could maintain a pretense for another month or so, weave the things I'd learned at inpatient into my conversations to make me seem trustworthy, then I would be on my way to Phase 2 and another step closer to a clean rap sheet.

But then I learned that I had been assigned to a new counselor. Great. A new person whom I needed to win over.

Bruce was an old hat at this substance use disorder thing. He spent his career in California, primarily in the Silicon Valley area. He was an old-school 12-Stepper of the AA ilk—the comparatively clean-cut and well-to-do original 12-steppers. Don't get me wrong, he was as junkie as it gets during his using days, but he was decidedly on the traditional 12-Step side. On the other side, the NA (Narcotics Anonymous) stereotype consists of the face-tattooed, formerly incarcerated, juvenile detention, baby-mama-daddy folks. That wasn't Bruce—he had a bachelor's degree in political science and spent most of his homeless time sleeping on the beaches of Hawaii. When he got clean and sober, he decided to study the science of addiction deeply and, after paying his dues at Medicaid-funded community service providers, graduated to working with the Silicon Valley set, counseling over-stimulated overachievers who needed to self-medicate to keep up with the Musk and Zuckerberg worshippers.

Now, here Bruce was, in a rural, somewhat economically depressed county, working for a community agency that served criminal drug addicts of the NA set.

I didn't feel so alone anymore. I was the only Drug Court participant in my cohort who was college-educated, came from outside Kitsap County, had a corporate career, and was somewhere between 15 and 20 years older than most of my Drug Court classmates, constantly feeling out of place and trying to fit in.

Good. I could get Bruce on my side much more easily than I had feared.

Rather than walking the streets at night and giving money away, I gave the casinos my money. Kitsap County Drug Court prohibits its participants from crossing county lines, as we're required to serve our time in the community rather than prison, so the court wants to keep tabs on us. I had a car that cost $100K brand new and was still flashy after 15 years of service, so the confines of county lines didn't even cross my mind.

During one of my many cross-county treks, I won $500 on one spin, looked at my phone, and saw a message from Amelia, one of the many call girls who would let me stay at her motel room while her man was away, shooting me up with meth, and then shoo me away when she expected her man to return. I always wanted to hook up with her, and it was evident that she was interested. But I was living on the streets when we met, so I was always too poor to seal the deal.

AMELIA: "Wya? Wyd?"

I messaged back a long description of what had happened to me, including hitting the unemployment jackpot.

AMELIA: "Omg I'm so proud of you. Come see me."

Amelia stayed at the Extended Stay Suites near the end of the Highway on the Fife end, with Tacoma just on the other side of the Fishing Wars Memorial Bridge. The cash in my pockets was burning a hole, and my mouth watered at the prospect of seeing Amelia.

The traffic light at the intersection south of the Little Queen turned yellow, so I floored the gas of my V8 German sedan to beat the light.

Upon entering Amelia's room, which was uncomfortably stuffed to the gills, she gave me a big hug. I took the $500 out of my pocket and set it down on the kitchen counter. She counted the money and let out a tiny squeal. I asked to use her bathroom, and while inside, I took a little baggie containing Wellbutrin powder, used the straw I had handy in my pocket, and snorted all the contents from the baggie. I then took a Viagra pill from the same pocket and bit half of it off.

That's as exciting as the night got.

I was so uncomfortable. Amelia was smoking blues (fentanyl) to get in the mood, then trying on her little cat costumes to arouse me. I was stuck on her bed, rigid (my body, not my cock), staring at the television. Amelia began experiencing sympathetic discomfort, standing a few feet from the bed, her eyes fixed on the television. We didn't have anything to say to each other. I was so used to her hitting me with a needle and getting me aroused that way that I didn't know what to do without the high. Amelia eventually locked herself in the bathroom. I was terrified. Without meth, I'd lost my ability to get aroused.

In the end, I silently slunk out of her room.

A few weeks later, I received a piece of mail from Fife Traffic Enforcement. It was a red-light ticket. I would later discover that, like parking tickets, they don't show up on your record. At the time, I thought the right thing to do (and I wanted to do the right thing, sometimes) was to come clean and tell Laurel about it. Drug Court appreciated the gesture.

Nevertheless, Drug Court's goal was to develop different habits in me, so I was put on surveillance for two months—an ankle monitor to track my whereabouts and an 8 pm curfew. To this day, I feel uncomfortable being out later than 9 pm—nothing good usually happens after that hour.

During those forced early nights, I implemented one of the tenets I learned from Codependent No More: goals cure boredom. It was summertime; the sun hadn't fully set by curfew, so I spent what would have been unbearably boring evenings—which are dangerous moments full of urges for people in early recovery—developing my vision of a startup that would purchase the rundown motels that had been welcomed respite on the streets, and in which I had recently been unable to have sex with a lovely little call girl because I wasn't high, to renovate into transitional housing for the homeless. I would fund it by encouraging national retailers to redirect the charitable donations they are obligated to give away and provide them with loss prevention services.

I told Laurel about my vision—the first person to whom I pitched the idea concretely and eloquently.

"That's amazing. And it'll support you through retirement."

Chapter 8

Phase II

It took me six months to finish Phase 1—double the minimum time. But I would sail through Phase 2, that is, it would take me four months, the minimum allotted time.

A lot of stuff was packed into that short period of my life. I'd start MRT (Moral Reconation Therapy) and, after a rough start, surpass most of the participants who had begun the program ahead of me. I would reconnect with my birth family, and in fundamental ways, actually connect with them for the first time. Finally, I would embark on the continuing journey of overcoming the shame of my addiction and the consequences that it had created in my life by appropriating the derogatory power of internet shaming.

I also began incorporating my vision for a socially conscious startup into any conversation where it might fit. As I write this, I can hear the first tête-à-tête with my publisher about the approach I had initially intended to use for this book—one part dark and racy memoir, and the other part business book. He suggested that the business book stand alone—the follow-up to this memoir. I recognized his wisdom and fully intended to follow his guidance. But I also see just how fundamental my startup vision has been to my recovery. It was the goal that I would turn to by default to cure the perilous boredom that would inevitably descend upon me, propping up my confidence, which was at its nadir, as my current predicament as a lowly prison diversion-program participant was nakedly transparent to my Drug Court team, every other program participant, seemingly to the entire South Kitsap County community, and my birth family.

My startup vision allowed me to refer to myself as a promising startup founder, while giving me a subject to leverage as a conversation piece without resorting to unsavory details about my current lifestyle (Oxford House, Drug Court, EBT cards, rental assistance...in short, post-criminal poverty). Above all, my vision provided me with the vehicle to transform my shameful past into my personal brand.

So, I need to talk about it.

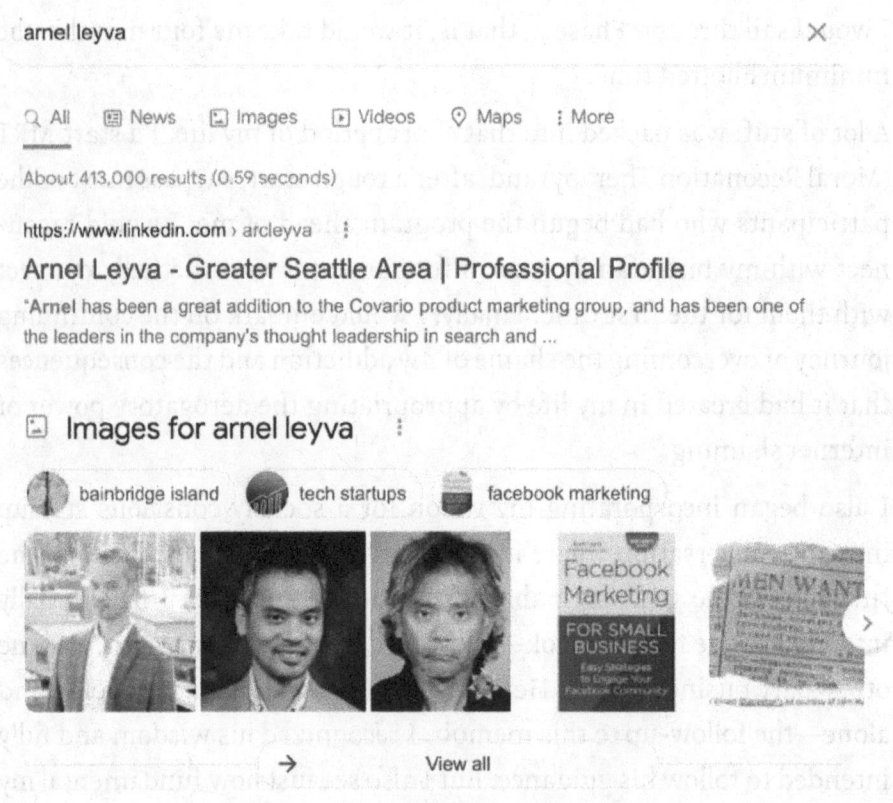

"Oh, shit." I felt a darkness darker than embarrassment, but I couldn't find the words.

In 2021, Google search results featured a layout that displayed images from around the internet to create a collage-style listing, positioned below the top listing. The search listings screenshot on the previous page was served to Bruce's laptop after he looked up my name at my behest.

My intention was to show off. During one of our weekly counseling sessions, I recounted stories of how I used the online presence that I had nurtured since 2003 to close deals with women at marketing conferences, Craigslist Casual Encounters, and escort sites. I owned my name online—my LinkedIn profile, created during the company's first year of existence, industry articles published in my name, the business book I had been paid to write—I was a big deal. And then I saw it: my mugshot from the road trip with FU-Guy to Portland.

After the counseling session, I went home with my tail between my legs.

How the Google crawler usually finds criminal booking photos is as follows:

1. Law enforcement agencies release mugshots and arrest details to local newspapers and other media.
2. Websites search local newspapers for mugshots to post on their own websites.
3. Google usually serves these websites as the top results when a person's name is looked up on search engines.

But my arrest wasn't a big media thing, so I wanted to determine how that particular booking photo, and not the numerous other photos that had come before it, was crawled and served. After conducting some research, I discovered that this random dude's hobby was to post booking photos of fugitives from justice who had been picked up in the Portland area.

MRT and Brené Brown would show me how to develop a strategy to reappropriate my mugshot for my personal benefit.

**

"Is there anything else?" Laurel ended every session with this question.

"I can't tell you everything."

"Why not?" She wasn't amused.

"Um...because not everything is everybody's business."

"Have you ever heard of lying by omission?"

"I understand the words. But I do not agree with them," was my definitive answer.

"I'm going to start you on MRT earlier than usual."

MRT sessions were held once per week on Fridays. As I described in an earlier chapter, it took me four attempts to get over myself and stop being a jerk long enough to pass the first step—the Testimony. Each step contains an essence that participants must memorize and recite before presenting the associated homework to the group...

1. Honesty
2. Trust
3. Acceptance
4. Awareness
5. Healing damaged relationships
6. Helping others
7. Long-term goals and identity
8. Short-term goals and consistency
9. Commitment to change
10. Maintaining positive change
11. Keeping moral commitments
12. Choosing moral goals.

The goal is to become Normal in the ways developmental psychologists propose that all human beings naturally develop if given the safe and encouraging environment required to fulfill their innate potential. Thus, MRT leads traumatized criminal addicts through the nurturing process they never received in childhood.

I went to see Carol because I was confused about what to do with these emotions—in fact, I didn't know what I was feeling until she told me, "It's shame."

I had never named it.

Carol suggested that I watch Brené Brown's TED Talk (which blew her up) and read some of her work.

Brené Brown describes shame as the painful emotion signifying your unworthiness of love and belonging. It dreads disconnection and detests being defined by words, so people overcome with shame usually avoid expressing it. In this silence, shame appropriates even more power. The antidote is shame resilience, which has four components:

1. Recognizing, naming, and understanding our shame triggers

Carol helped me with this one—like I said, I didn't even know that I was experiencing shame when I saw those Google search results in Bruce's office; all of the sudden, I was disconnected from the image I had of myself, the 1175 followers on LinkedIn, and the prospect of ever regaining a normal life, but this experience led to a connection of who I had always been yet had hidden in a double life, which reached its apotheosis while I was on the streets.

2. Identifying external factors that led to feelings of shame

Those would be…Google search results displaying to the world what I had been up to in Portland; thinking about what others who had known me in my previous life would think when they saw that mugshot; every time I thought about my current situation—a court-ordered participant in a prison diversion program, living with a bevy of justice system-involved dudes in an old halfway house, subsisting on unemployment after a high-earning career, unable to get sexually turned on without drugs, and never learning how to have healthy relationships.

3. Connecting with others to receive and offer empathy

As I was disciplined about doing my MRT homework, I quickly moved up to Step 5: Healing damaged relationships; I had been avoiding my father's prodding to reconnect with the rest of the family—he had engaged in this campaign since I left the streets, but I continued accusing my siblings of being judgmental, so I stayed away; shame was holding me back, so I agreed to a reunion on Thanksgiving, which always falls on or around the birthday that my father and I share: November 25th; I made this agreement in the face of overwhelming feelings of unworthiness—I thought myself unworthy of my family's love, and the Google search results proved it, yet I followed Ms. Brown's instructions in the face of fear.

4. Speaking about our feelings of shame with others

If I could tell my story to the world as the lived experience serving as the foundation that informs my socially conscious startup, then no one could ever use my past against me, so I decided to turn my shame into my personal brand—I would reemerge on LinkedIn, which I had quit since descending into the underground, by publishing an article that would tell my story; I was scared shitless, which meant that this was my task.

* * *

The first sibling to contact me was my younger brother, Dennis.

He invited me to dinner. We chose a restaurant near his place in South Lake Union, near Amazon's headquarters. I had to ask Drug Court's permission to cross county lines. They readily gave it, as I was reconnecting with one of my family members.

During dinner, we began the conversation by showing each other the watches we had acquired—Steve McQueen wore mine in the car racing movie Le Mans, and his was the same one worn by the latest James Bond. This interaction should give you a sense of our relationship. We were still caught up in the race and had more than a modicum of competition between us. The conversation turned to drugs (I introduced him to the hard stuff when we were younger).

"Even though meth was the drug that precipitated my downfall, it is so much better for sex than cocaine. I mean, I can actually get a hard-on," I confessed.

"I've never had any problems with that on coke," Dennis boasted.

"Bro, that's like, a superpower." I was amazed…and jealous.

Here my younger brother was, living in a condominium in the heart of the Amazon district, which he had purchased about a decade earlier (so it must have had a stack of equity), working for a tech company in sales and pulling a fat salary, still doing drugs without having ruined his life, and he could get it up on coke.

I wondered what was wrong with me that I couldn't handle my drugs like that. I knew I had an incurable addiction that I needed to manage like a chronic disease—that much I had learned in inpatient treatment and weekly outpatient sessions—and that, while normies can do drugs on weekends, I do drugs until I'm homeless. That's the true measure of the difference. So, I wasn't thinking that I could take up drugs again without ruining my life. But how could my younger brother, who bathed in the same gene pool that produced this drug addict, continue living The Life without becoming a societal pariah?

What I would find out about Dennis, just as with every addict, was that he was not special, and my recovery journey would become the catalyst for him to begin his own.

The next sibling to get in touch was my youngest sister, El. She is a registered nurse, working mainly in the long hours of the emergency room—our shared upbringing manifested in her as a predilection toward workaholism in an adrenaline-fueled environment. In many ways, I was closest to her amongst all of my four sisters. She looked up to me, and I consistently let her down. I represent precisely the type of narcissistic men she had attracted and was attracted to, until she met her current husband, after having done a lot of work on herself to find her true core.

I didn't realize just how much internal work she and my other sisters had done while I was supporting my double life, and then, without a second thought, going all out and gallivanting full-time in the underground, until I reunited with my family. So, when El texted me, I was on guard. As was she. We played text tag, trying to find a meeting time and place. We finally settled on lunch at a restaurant in West Seattle, where she and her husband lived. Again, I had to ask permission from Drug Court, and again they obliged because I was fully working MRT Step 5.

When I arrived at the restaurant, El was still on her way, so I took a seat and waited. When she entered, I didn't recognize her; it had been so long. But she recognized me immediately and began to tear up.

"I don't trust you," El stated, after we had ordered our food. "I see people like you all the time in the ER. You'll say whatever you need to get what you want, especially prescription drugs."

"I preferred street drugs," I wisecracked. El's forthrightness took me aback. I didn't remember her having set boundaries. "Seriously, though, I can't make you trust me. All I can do is the next right thing, if I can figure out what that is."

I surprised myself with that response. I'd heard it in one of my outpatient sessions. Whoever said it had for sure heard it in an AA or NA meeting. But it rang true for me nonetheless, and it seemed the right thing to say during that lunch with El. She softened after I said those words—not that she trusted me suddenly, but I think she knew that I had at the very least begun to accept the change process.

A couple of months after those initial meetings, the day of the family reunion finally arrived, and in 2021, Thanksgiving fell on the same day as my father's and my birthday.

My younger sister, Maridelle (between me and El), was hosting. I'd say that I was most competitive with Maridelle—we are the most alike in how we organize our thoughts (our texts can include enumerated lists of points and to-dos), and we are the closest in age. Maridelle is also the most financially successful of all my siblings, so as much as I wanted to discount her accomplishments as the product of having sold herself to the suburban lifestyle that I swore off with my double life, half of that double life had been invested in upholding a suburban front. Maridelle's mere existence held up a mirror to my hypocrisy.

When I arrived at Maridelle's swanky apartment next to Google's Seattle complex in South Lake Union, she opened the door and started tearing up. That moment represented the beginning of our healing together. I discovered that she had assumed the role of kin keeper—working to keep the family connected by sharing news, planning and hosting gatherings, helping family members stay in touch, and providing emotional and financial support to my disabled mother who was cared for by my father, as well as maintaining and passing on family traditions, values, and histories—all while becoming a Reiki master and secretly working on launching her own tech business.

Everyone welcomed me with open arms. I wasn't sure I deserved this.

For the first time in nearly a decade, I saw my mother in person, not behind a facemask tucked away in a car, since she suffered a brain aneurysm. I was afraid to talk to her.

Growing up, my mother was controlling and meddling, at least, that's how I experienced it. When her dementia was still fresh, I marveled at how Zen she had become. She was in the moment, relearning how her body functioned, but memories from deep in the past would also resurface, while she couldn't remember what happened an hour ago.

But now, significant parts of her old personality had returned, and I didn't know how to take it. I was used to being on guard with her, waiting for the usual criticism about my life choices that would send me into a spiral. Now, her emotional palette had regressed to primary colors, though she could also unintentionally say something that might come from a yogi on a mountain top. Perhaps the aneurysm peeked open her third eye.

Lastly, there was my father.

He had kept tabs on me while I was on the streets. Twice, I met up with him and my mother at the Issaquah Park Transit Center during the height of COVID and my criminal homelessness—both times, he gave me a wad of cash in an envelope. I know that those interactions were a way to assuage his guilt for what I had become. The shame of taking multiple buses to get from the Highway to Issaquah was no match for the desperation that drove me. My father eventually stopped giving me money at the urging of my siblings, as they recognized that his gifts only served to enable my addiction.

I absolutely spent most of that money on ounces of meth, but that money also replaced my stolen phones twice, ensuring that he wouldn't lose touch with me. I can honestly say that when he finally declined to give me more money, I didn't resent him, even in the throes of my addiction.

During the Thanksgiving reunion, on our shared birthday, my father saw me in person without a face mask for the first time in nearly a decade.

My oldest sister, Arminda, lives in Vancouver, BC, so she wasn't at the reunion. She, her husband Bob, and son Nick were the only family members with whom I actively kept in touch during my estrangement—Armi's own estrangement from our family made us brother and sister in arms, as it were. The three of them were the first to witness what I had become on the streets. At the end of my first year of homelessness, I met them at Dick's Burgers in Queen Anne. I confessed to being a criminal. Bob asked whether I had actually been convicted. Armi gave me $200. I was wearing a brand-new (boosted) pair of Marshall headphones around my neck and gave them to Nick as a Christmas gift. It had taken a couple days of plotting and working up my courage to pilfer them. They were my prized possession at the time, so it really was the absolute best I had to offer.

My older sister, Nell (between Armi and me), was out of town with her partner during the Thanksgiving reunion at Maridelle's. I wouldn't see her until she hosted Christmas dinner at her condominium in downtown Kirkland. She also teared up when I entered her kitchen, where she was putting the finishing touches on an extravagant dinner.

Nell and I shared the black sheep designation in our family. We used to party together, but it didn't take her down the way it did me. She had been married and divorced twice. I would set up a weekly call with Nell, an activity Bruce had suggested during one of our counseling sessions, as a way to involve my family more deeply in my recovery journey. Nell had done work on herself while I was gone, and she had finally found a partner who didn't give her the feeling that she could do better—she had found her equal, which meant that she had gotten to know herself and what she wanted in another.

But I didn't know anything about the journeys my siblings had traversed to arrive at that point in our lives, signified by Christmas dinner. I was just as overwhelmed as I was at Thanksgiving and needed a way to decompress. At the dinner table, my siblings started discussing the types of wines they enjoyed.

"That wine is an acquired taste," Dennis stated. "I didn't use to like it."

"I think you either like something or don't," I judged.

"That's not true," El countered. "I didn't like sushi as a kid, but now I love it."

"Hmm. You're right. Just like I couldn't stand the taste of meth, but then I grew to love it."

The table erupted in laughter.

That night, when I returned to my Oxford House in Bremerton, I decided it was time to reemerge on LinkedIn and build my personal-professional brand on the open truth.

- Dec 2021 -

Last year, I was homeless for Thanksgiving and Christmas...this year, I was with my family for the holidays for the first time in 25 years. After a significant career in tech, I spent two years living on the streets hustling for drugs. I distilled the following market requirement while embedded in the frontline of the homelessness crisis:

"Making urban streets and business districts cleaner and safer will increase EVERYONE's quality of life and requires the supply of no-cost supportive housing to OUTPACE the growth of homeless encampments."

I spent this year developing a business plan to house entrenched homeless populations in motels renovated into no-cost supportive housing. A socially conscious Real Estate Investment Trust (REIT) underpins a sustainable business model by securitizing startup venture capital with property rights.

The only way I can manifest my vision of housing 1500 Seattle-area homeless addicts in five years is to tell my story. I want to thank the LinkedIn community for giving me the platform to overcome my shame and do just that. It's given me a newfound freedom.

My socially conscious startup's business model would evolve over the three years between writing this post and launching my startup. My further education at Olympic College in the Substance Use Disorder Professional program would give me a new lens on the type of housing that most effectively suits recovery for drug addicts. The reunification with my birth family increased my capacity for containing my shame—the shame didn't get smaller; I grew bigger.

My shame was a treasure.

Chapter 9

Phase III

Leading a double life is an addiction in itself.

Having cultivated such a life over my entire adulthood, stopping the behavior, no matter how much progress I'd made in my development as a human being, proved fruitless.

Here's some insight into the front I'd successfully constructed for my Drug Court team.

At the end of 2021, I wrote an unsolicited essay, "Arnel Leyva 2.0 [Beta Release]," representing my ascension to Phase 3. I submitted the essay to my Drug Court team, emailing it to Laurel, Bruce, Carol, and even Judge H. That was a bold move, but I thought so highly of what I'd written that I wanted to distribute it to as broad an audience as possible. The first part of the essay demonstrates my developing ability to examine my past behaviors from a maturing perspective, albeit with threads of bravado woven throughout the prose, while harkening back to my roots in the tech industry...

beta release

> *noun*
>
> *1 a Beta Release is a new version of a software program that contains all required features and has been put through a complete test cycle during which no bugs that crash the system, hang the application, or cause a loss of data were found. Before officially launching the new version, a beta version is released to a subset of the customer base, allowing it to be fully tested for bugs using a broad and unscripted approach.*

***

In New Year's past, I'd do one of these write-ups for myself in a vain attempt to control my destiny; to make myself feel better after spending the unreal week between Christmas Day and New Year's Day looking back in anger and judgment. I'd get high enough to feel better about a year invariably filled with seething regret and resentment that I hadn't acknowledged, but not so high that I'd lose control. I knew just how much dopamine I needed to feel good enough to focus. What I never realized until my first year of Drug Court was that I have been on my destiny's path along...no thanks to my control-freakedness.

When I was released from Kitsap County Jail 29 December 2020, I never imagined that I'd still be at the same Oxford House after one year, writing another one of my unsolicited essays to my Drug Court team as a token of my allegiance, and looking forward to acknowledging my first clean and sober birthday in a couple weeks.

What's different about this particular year-end essay is that I'm carrying very little judgment. Didn't have to force myself either. It's just happening naturally. My ability to assign the right weight to each unlikely event that led me here has created an environment where I don't feel an overwhelming urge to control the future. Instead, I'm comfortable naming this feeling exactly what it is and not crushing it with unrealistic expectations. It's Hope.

While representing a look back at the year just ending and a look forward to the coming year, this essay also represents my project work for the final week of 2021. My project is much more than launching my business. It's about incubating Arnel 2.0.

The start of 2022 marks the beta release of the next version of me.

The middle section of the essay recounts events from 2021; since these were covered in the previous chapter, I won't include them here. In the final section, the warring factions within me reveal their colors. The beginning of the final section draws on content from a book I was reading then, *The Molecule of More*, by Daniel Z. Lieberman and Michael E. Long...

Everything boils down to Dopamine and Serotonin.

Desire Dopamine stems from the most primitive part of our brain. It drives us to want more and more and more. It drives romance and addiction, both of which are modern manifestations of humanity's basic urge to gather resources in the pursuit of making our future existence more likely. Our brains are programmed to crave the unexpected and thus to look to the future, where every exciting possibility begins.

Being in love fades because romance is powered by dopamine, whereas serotonin allows us to enjoy mundane love. The Desire Dopamine rush of the chase fades over an 18-month period. That's why all my romantic relationships have ended within two years. That's also why I never held a job for more than two years—the professional romance couldn't last.

Furthermore, drugs act as artificial dopamine rushes, and since primal dopamine is all about the getting, there is never any satisfaction (which comes from serotonin).

I've been a slave to primal dopamine all of my life.

The architecture of the Drug Court program leverages serotonin and the control (or mature) version of dopamine to develop satisfaction in the present and hope, underpinned by pragmatic strategies, for the future. I'm learning to rely on the mature control of the dopamine manufactured in the most evolved area of the brain, as well as the enjoyment of the serotonin manufactured in the rarest part of the brain, to neutralize the overwhelmingly addictive urges driven by Desire Dopamine.

The Drug Court education takes place within the 18-month romance period. So, by the time I'm over Drug Court, the program will have given me the tools to be mindful in the present while having faith in the future.

I'm a spiritual being in a carbon-based body driven by chemical reactions, experiencing an emotional existence perpetuated by the drive to secure the future.

And then there's the last part...

A great man does not seek to lead...he hears the call to lead and answers it.

(Just watched Dune version 2021)

It's enough that I finally like the person I've become.

I'm aware I'm continually becoming the man I always knew I could be.

If I continue respecting myself, I have no choice but to answer my calling.

When I was an uninformed codependent unaware of the outsized influence that Desire Dopamine had on my behavior, I never understood my penchant for overdelivering during my first year on the job, and then petulantly under-delivering the second year. With increasing self-awareness, I don't see that behavior going unchecked. My second year in Drug Court will be different from the patterns of my second year in professional romantic relationships. Same with personal ones (when I'm ready).

The beta version of Arnel 2.0 has been officially released. Metaphorically testing for and identifying leftover bugs will, in practice, entail getting myself mentally, emotionally, and physically ready to answer the call of my calling. If I focus on those elements, the financial aspect will fall into place.

I'm not tripping about under-delivering this year. You know why? Because I have the support of a corporation like Drug Court, love and trust in myself, and faith in a power greater than any of us.

I have to do this. It's my destiny.

What a load of shit.

Okay, that's probably an unfair assessment of my "beta" version. A load of bugs remained in my programming that needed to be identified through testing and then fixed. While I was writing the above essay, I also engaged in crushing, cutting, and snorting my Wellbutrin prescription…every day; I would speed in my car at 100 miles per hour at least once a day; and sneak to the casinos at least once a week. I also thought that working the MRT steps meant that I had transcended the need to work the 12 Steps properly, so I sent premature amends letters to my siblings, old friends, and my last corporate boss — really, everyone I had mentioned in my MRT Step 1 Testimony.

I messaged Ava with my amends, acknowledging that I had made promises I knew I would never keep.

We started hanging out again, seeing each other about once a week, with the majority of our second time around spent on Messenger.

01/22/2022, 10:29 PM

AVA: "Heyy. Wyd?"

ME: "About to go to bed. I got outpatient group tomorrow morning. What's up wichu?"

AVA: "I'm just sitting here missing u missing the old dayzzz."

ME: "Old dayzzz?"

AVA: "♡ at a hotel."

ME: "We gotta get past the old days. We learned from them. But yeah, I like you better now than before."

AVA: "So do I. I wish we could have that shit now instead of then."

ME: "It came at a steep price. Like I actually think it's a blessing that I'm forced to sell my car bc I haven't felt comfortable driving it for a while now. It's too showy. I don't want to be a showoff anymore. It feels fake. After that speeding ticket, I just hope drug court sends me to defensive driving class instead of taking my keys.

AVA: "I hope so too lol. I stayed at this dude's house who was trying to be my sugar daddy. I made him take me back to my mom's tho. He is really annoying. Omfg. Like he is so obnoxious and annoying, and he doesn't want to cough up any cash at all and all he does is micromanage me and complain about every little thing I do. Its unbearable."

ME: "Was I that bad at first? Probably lol."

AVA: "NO. Not at all. Not ever. And when u were, u fucking made up for it and it was rare. And it was probably called for."

ME: "If I had the power to give you anything in the world, anything at all, it would be a map showing you the way to your independence. To do something that gives you a purpose and pays the rent and bills. To be out from under anyone's thumb. To know which responsibilities are yours and not be burdened by those that aren't yours to carry. To NOT have to put up with stupid-ass dudes trying to control you ever again. Never ever again. To know that you can have the freedom to DO YOU always... the first step is to decide to make that your goal every day. Love you girl."

AVA: "Xoxo love you too. So, car dates just out of the question now?"

ME: "We're too emotionally close to just be like that. At least I obviously can't."

AVA: "Dang lol."

ME: "Come on. You were there. And it was partly your vibe. Right? Plus, you know my money is messed up rn, so even if I wanted to again… since my unemployment stopped in Sept, I've been living off my savings. That's the real reason I'm going back to school. Financial aid."

AVA: "Xp it wasn't my vibe! I was totally feeding off yours xD. And ya, you're broke."

ME: "The first thing you said was you're just getting done with your period so just head and I'm all um love you too lol."

AVA: "LMAO. Okay, I'm done. So, maybe you can help find me another sugar??

ME: "I'm not tryna be your manager."

AVA: "Xp I do need to pick up some suboxone from this girl. She said to meet her at the supercenter parking lot. So could you give me a ride?"

ME: "I'll let you know when I get to your parents. Dude. It's so weird. We used to wait in the same parking lot for your old connect and now we're doing the same thing but with subs. I still don't understand why the clinic won't put you on them legally."

AVA: It's stupid. They wanna put me on methadone. No way. Lemme know when ur outside.

01/30/2022, 7:49 PM

ME: "If you ever think about going to college, you'd be eligible for all tuition paid and about three grants for books, laptop and living expenses. I'm going to get a substance use disorder professional certificate so I can prepare for running shelters and supportive housing. I should get some financial aid. Not as much as you bc I already have a bachelor's degree, but I'll get enough to not have to get a job. School will be my job. You are smart and intelligent. Sharp as a razor with innate empathy that makes you caring and humane. Use your talents... https://www.olympic.edu

AVA: "I wanna do massage therapy. I gotta go to school for that right ???"

ME: "To get the level of financial aid I showed you earlier, you gotta go to a community college or university. Massage therapy is private and not covered the same way. You could be a physical therapist though. That's covered."

AVA: "Thank you tho."

ME: "Ok, I'll stop tryna run your life now lol."

AVA: "I don't mind u running my life lol."

02/02/2022, 12:01 PM

ME: Check it out.

https://medium.com/@arnel_3794/homeless-vs-neighbors-21st-century-class-warfare-waged-on-the-battleground-of-parking-lots-6e8ca1c3a685

Homeless vs. Neighbors: 21st Century Class Warfare Waged on the Battleground of Parking Lots

AVA: "I just read it. Go back and re-read it. You need to edit some shit lol. But it's great."

ME: "Like what?"

AVA: "Just some typos. But also...I feel like maybe you should re-order it all another way."

ME: "Tell me."

AVA: "Like...I see how putting your story first would make sense...but I think you should start It by briefly explaining the problems we all see with homelessness and then state how to fix it… It all makes sense without knowing ur background… But I think that ur story NEEDS to be a part of it. I think IT should be near the end…after reading ur ideas about it all on a FACTUAL basis…then tell ur story and it'll just make the facts even more real."

ME: "I'm tryna understand how reordering it would be more beneficial. No offense taken. I'm not offended. I hope for this type of feedback."

AVA: "I feel like the way ur presenting it is making it more about YOU than the actual homelessness and how to fix it…"

ME: "Oh…just thinking out loud…you're saying I should talk about how I gained this knowledge after explaining the research and analysis. Right?"

AVA: "Yes…I am not saying NOT to tell ur story…it NEEDS to be in there. Just don't make it the very first thing. Lol"

ME: "It's funny. I've been told to tell my story to get over my shame. I had the hardest time telling my story…I couldn't even include it in the end. But I got over my shame by putting my story front and center. Now I can chill a little bit lol."

AVA: "I love it."

ME: "Ok you're gonna be my editor as I write my memoir…bc you'll keep me in check and help make sure it sells to Gen Z."

AVA: "Lol I got chu."

02/07/2022, 2:37 PM

AVA: "YO. CAN U PLEASE PLEASE COME GET ME I NEED TO GO GET MY KID."

ME: "I can't. I'm on a 12 Step Zoom meeting that I have to do and then I have to take a UA."

AVA: "BABY DAD IS SMOKED TF OUT BEING CRAZY AF. I can't stop crying."

ME: "I can't leave right now. And I can't get in the middle of you guys again."

AVA: Sorry I am frantic. My mom can't do it or my dad. IT'S NOT GETTING IN THE MIDDLE OF SHIT. IT'S TAKING ME TO PROTECT MY SON. WTF. This has LITERALLY never happened before. FML. I hate my life."

ME: "Are you alright?"

AVA: "Not really."

ME: "I'm not sure if you've noticed, but I've become a lot better at coping with things that used to automatically make me frantic. I trip less often on things that were once unmanageable for me. One of the things that has helped me to chill and gain control over myself in situations is having a community of people who've been through it and provide examples that I can emulate. I'm going to an NA meeting tonight if you want to try it out. Lmk."

AVA: "Ok. Yea I'll prob come. No, wait. My kid just got dropped off."

02/24/2022, 5:49 PM

ME: Just sold the Audi in an all-cash deal. Tomorrow I'm going to our old haunt Aurora to pick up a Saab."

AVA: "YAY."

ME: "Change of plans. Omw to Tacoma not Aurora to get another Audi. Smaller and better gas mileage. I didn't tell drug court. Just a quick trip. What they don't know won't hurt them."

AVA: "Lol. HEY. I got approved for the rental assistance thing thru Kitsap Community Resources and I'm getting 32 months of rent paid ALL AT ONCE."

ME: I love KCR... they've been covering me for seven months now."

02/25/2022, 7:06 PM

ME: "I didn't get the car. Just didn't feel right. Now I'm stuck in Tacoma. I have to spend the night in a motel bc by the time the next bus to Seattle comes, I'll miss the last ferry to Bremerton."

AVA: "Uber?"

ME: "Uber would cost more than a motel. This room is kinda triggering me lol."

AVA: "Call me when u can."

ME: "Wow. I checked Uber and it's only $70. I got outta here with a refund and am waiting for my Uber."

AVA: "Good job love."

03/08/2022, 2:26 PM

AVA: "I got a suboxone appointment w/ a Seattle doctor over the phone. It's kind of a scam thing my friend hooked me up with…it's a real doctor but she's really lenient n just writes the script no prob don't even ever have to actually go into the office for a checkup."

ME: "Not a scam thing. It serves a big gap in the market for people like you. There's lots of them. ADHD prescriptions have a similar thing. I should know."

AVA: "Yay it's amazing. No more spending money on it by this time next week."

03/15/2022, 3:32 PM

AVA: "I'm out boosting right now u need anything????"

ME: "No. I won't deliberately put you in a vulnerable position for my benefit. But thanks for thinking of me lol."

AVA: LMAO!!!!!

03/28/2022, 3:23 PM

ME: "Drug Court did a surprise house visit on me. They found the plate I use to snort my Wellbutrin in my nightstand. It was caked with it, plus a straw, razor blade, and credit card. They went through my phone and saw the stuff about going to Tacoma and there were also those messages about boosting, so I was sent to jail Wednesday until today. It's called a Drug Court weekend. Now I've got to do another stint at an inpatient facility. I didn't relapse on street drugs but what they call an emotional relapse exhibiting addict behavior."

AVA: "Are you serious? I'm sorry. Love you. Hit me up when you can talk…xo"

ME: "Not your fault. I just can't be a part of your life if the way you choose to support yourself includes boosting. I could hide it but I'm not going to hide anything anymore that doesn't align with my values. Take care."

AVA: "Lol yea I knew this was going to happen eventually."

* * *

When I arrived at the American Behavioral Health Services (ABHS) inpatient treatment facility in Port Angeles, I was stuck, not quite ready to leave every facet of The Life behind.

"You want some Wellbutrin?" The guy who went through the intake process with me that day shall henceforth be referred to as Wellbutrin Guy.

I had given him a cigarette when we were allowed to take our first break after the arduous intake process. He didn't have any cigarettes, nor did he have many possessions. I arrived prepared with two cartons of cigarettes, so I had just given him a pack.

"You got some?" I was pleasantly surprised.

"Yeah. It's the least I can do. Hold on." Wellbutrin Guy's dorm room was across the hall, so he went back to his room and returned in no time with three pills.

"Keep a lookout," I ordered.

I crushed a pill without removing the coating. I hadn't used Wellbutrin in any way, shape, or form since Drug Court ordered me to stop getting my prescription filled, and I'd flushed the remnants of my last bottle down the toilet.

This line gave me a bump rivalling cocaine.

Wellbutrin Guy stood at the threshold of my door, as we chopped it up like a coke jag—he led a deliberately transient life, one inpatient treatment facility to another, laying low after getting caught snitching on some dangerous dudes, fashioning for himself his very own identity protection program. Before arriving at ABHS, he led a relatively normal life in a transition housing community in downtown Seattle. Then, Wellbutrin Guy overheard a new tenant talking about the people supposedly stalking him. The paranoia was too much, pushing him to relapse, so he slinked back to the safety of yet another addiction treatment facility.

My sympathy for him superseded my suspicion that his half-life was no longer about actual bad dudes pursuing him, but all in his head. I gave him another pity pack of cigarettes.

"Bro, lemme get you a couple more pills. We could keep doing this, you know."

"Totally."

For the next two weeks, Wellbutrin Guy fed me pills in exchange for cigarettes.

As Wellbutrin Guy's paranoia subsided, he entered my dorm room and sat on the empty bed across from me. I told him my recent story—getting expelled from my Oxford House for misusing my prescription; I didn't even really relapse; it wasn't my housemates who had made the decision; it was the outreach manager working for Oxford House corporate; at least he gave me three days to pack up my stuff.

On the last day at my first and only Oxford House, I found myself parked in front of the UPS Store next to Safeway in East Bremerton, thinking that if I was going to be punished for a quasi-relapse, I might as well go all out. Judge H was forcing me to redo Phase 3, which would add another five months to my sentence. A case of the fuck-its was ruminating within me and gaining momentum. What stopped me was an empty bank account and needing to attend classes to receive financial aid.

Instead of going on the run, I called Skye, the Catholic Community Services HEN (Housing and Essential Needs) program manager. She was the first person to whom I had shown the very first PowerPoint presentation illustrating my vision of a social service agency that housed drug addicts in the same run-down motels that exploited their housing instability and unworthiness as renters, just as I had experienced on the streets. She loved the idea, allowing me to use her as a reference for a grant application to the Amazon Housing Equity Fund, which was ultimately declined. Looking back, that was a stroke of luck—I'm sure that managing that much money so early in my recovery would have triggered a relapse.

I would visit Skye at the HEN office in downtown Bremerton from time to time to check on my progress on the housing assistance waiting list—every time, she would give me the harsh truth: unless I were truly homeless, I would remain at the bottom of the priority list. Having been kicked out of my Oxford House, mulling over my options of going on the run or I-did-not-know-what-else, I was well and truly homeless…again.

Skye sprang into action, putting me up in a room at a nearby motel with which HEN had a housing contract and assigning me to one of her case managers. I stayed in that room, replete with a Drug Court ankle monitor, until a bed in an addiction treatment facility became available. I was forced to drop out of Olympic College before the start of my first quarter.

During the first half of the inpatient program, I tried to be the overachiever in group classes. The treatment facility was court-ordered to provide progress reports on me, so I wanted to prove to Drug Court that they didn't need to worry about me ever again, all the while continuing to snort up a storm. I especially looked forward to mornings after med call—the combined effect of the new psych meds that my mental health prescriber had put me on as a replacement for Wellbutrin, a little Wellbutrin powder that I had prepared before bed and reserved for my morning ritual, a cup of coffee, and the first cigarette of the day, left me in a lovely stupor.

On one such morning, my inpatient drug counselor called me into her office for our weekly one-on-one session.

"You remind me a little bit of myself. You're too smart for your own good." She didn't blink.

"I'll take that as a compliment."

"It's harder for intelligent people to fully buy into recovery, to accept it wholeheartedly, because we think we know everything. So, for the next week, I want you to do an exercise. I want you to sit on your hands and shut your mouth during group."

My inpatient drug counselor's request turned out to be one of the most difficult exercises ever. I never realized how often I felt compelled to speak in a formal instructional setting, seemingly all the time, regardless of the context. I had a burning desire to raise my hand 90% of the time. When the desire was too strong to bear and I'd throw my hand in the air, my inpatient drug counselor would merely ignore me. Then, I would literally sit on my hands. But after a few days, sitting on my hands became perfunctory, ritualistic. I started noticing that I listened intently to the content of other people's shares—like I was honestly heeding what other people had to say, rather than formulating one of my patented profound comments as I waited for whoever was talking to stop blathering on and on.

In these moments, I would think about how much Ava could benefit from this setting. But she wasn't "using" anymore, so she would be ineligible for inpatient treatment. I tried persuading her to join an outpatient group, but just the thought of it seemed an imposition on her lifestyle. Trudging to an outpatient facility to sit around with a bunch of other addicts talking primarily about a load of shit can be a chore. But for me, it was a Drug Court requirement, so attend I did. Sometimes, someone would say something inadvertently profound that allowed me to forgive myself, and always, the group wrapped me in a like-minded community of people to hang with who were barely hanging onto the other side of addiction.

I noticed a gratitude for Drug Court well up inside me for the institutionalized (in the very best sense) external support that the program gave me. Ava didn't have that. I tried to provide a semblance of that support to her, but I was in no position to do for others what I still could not do for myself.

These thoughts formed a little angel on my shoulder when, halfway through my inpatient sojourn, I snorted a line of Wellbutrin for the last time. I don't remember if I started writing the amends letter to Drug Court, addressed to Laurel, the very day that I made the Determination—it might have been the following day—but write the letter I did, snitching on myself for all the violations I had committed over my first 16 months in the program, especially and including trading cigarettes for Wellbutrin. I mailed the letter and patted myself on the back, envisioning a humble and disciplined final two weeks at the inpatient facility. My countenance would be that of an all-around stand-up guy.

Instead, Drug Court instructed the treatment facility to extend my stay an extra week.

My inpatient drug counselor asked me to give up the identity of Wellbutrin Guy, which I finally understood was about accountability, not snitching. I asked her if she'd let me talk to him first, which she understood. Immediately following this little discussion, I tracked down Wellbutrin Guy and told him about the amends letter—he didn't get mad but was visibly scared, thinking that he'd be kicked out early for supplying prescription drugs to others, making him vulnerable to the baddies perpetually stalking him.

Unexpected words of wisdom came from my mouth—I urged him to come clean and not only would he not be kicked out, but he would most likely have his stay extended, because his co-occurring mental disorders were acute (I said that last part in my head—I didn't even know the word "acute" in clinical terms yet, but I knew that his disorders were way worse than mine).

That's exactly what happened for the exact reasons.

* * *

It had to be done.

After getting released from my second (and final) inpatient stint and then moving into a Homes of Compassion apartment on the border of East Bremerton and Silverdale, I made an appointment to see my mental health prescriber at PCHS (Peninsula Community Health Services). As a community agency, I was pleasantly surprised that they could schedule an appointment within a few days' notice—Medicaid-funded community agencies are notoriously overbooked and understaffed. I had been going to the same mental health prescriber almost from the start of my Drug Court career.

Before I left for ABHS, I went to see her about new meds, confessing that Drug Court had caught me snorting my prescription. My mental health prescriber burst into a short bout of laughter, then gathered herself, apologized, and assured me that I wasn't the first person.

"What can I do for you today?" She was sitting in front of the terminal and pulling up my file.

"I think we need to break up." I felt a sense of finality that was bittersweet.

"Okay." She tilted her head.

"You've helped me so much. Remember how you gave me that pep talk about my family last year? And you're not even my therapist. You laughed when I told you about snorting Wellbutrin. You didn't judge me. But if I leave here with a prescription for yet another psych med, then I will have succeeded in manipulating you into giving me something that I'm hoping will give me a little high."

"I think you're right. Good luck to you." She extended her hand, and I held it in a warm handshake.

I was scared shitless.

Sitting in my own room, in an apartment leased by a social service agency that provided long-term transitional housing, but not quite sober living, I had a newfound freedom. But I felt rudderless—no prescription drugs, no gambling, no hanging out with prostitutes—in short, no cross-addictions (except caffeine and nicotine). I didn't have anywhere to turn.

Almost a year and a half into "recovery," I had successfully managed to avert buying into the cult of the 12-Step Program, which seemed like a personal victory.

I had attended a few 12-Step meetings in person, but I didn't get to know people, nor want to, as they all seemed a bit too gung-ho about the whole thing. I had successfully avoided getting a sponsor, while doing most of my meetings online, especially on the website In the Rooms, which allows users to download a PDF attendance confirmation to show their compliance officers, and my paid version of Adobe Acrobat had given me the power to edit the dates and times on the PDFs to defraud the system. Since I had made the determination to invest in recovery fully, I couldn't fake it anymore.

I had nothing, so I decided to get an NA sponsor and do the steps for real.

Finding a sponsor is hard work. This person must be of the same gender to avoid unethical behavior between the sponsor, who has achieved stability in their life, and a vulnerable newcomer, who is susceptible to unscrupulous advances. So, no women (though this rule is mainly for predatory guys). This person should reside in the vicinity, enabling personal connections that are a hallmark of a supportive community. So, the cool guy who was part of a visiting NA fellowship at the ABHS facility was ruled out. No close friends or relatives, as previous relationships create ethical dilemmas regarding objectivity. I didn't have any close friends, and none of my relatives needed recovery, so no problem there.

I had one guy in mind, Scott—he was the Drug Court graduate who had given me a ride to the ABHS facility (Drug Court likes to recruit graduates to chaperon current participants to court-ordered appointments); he was well respected in the community; we had a good talk on the way to inpatient; he even let me park my car at his house while I was away; and he ran an NA meeting. But he already had a stable of sponsees, so I decided he was overbooked.

I planned to attend three separate weekly meetings around the area to start my sponsor dating. Plans fall apart—every time I'd pull into the parking lot of this or that church where a meeting was held, I'd experience a panic attack, sit in the parking lot to let it subside, and then drive away when the meeting started. After the last failed attempt, I attended Scott's meeting and asked him to be my sponsor. He accepted.

This section is another difficult one to write. As you'll see in the subsequent chapters, Scott became the co-founder of my social service agency—he stuck with me for almost two years before we landed our first sizable grant; his combined professional and volunteer experience in community building, which would be instrumental in winning the aforementioned grant, provided the yin to the yang of my business background and the clinical training in addiction treatment that I would eventually receive; he became a close friend and pivotal figure in my recovery, but we would eventually go through a business divorce driven by irreconcilable differences, so I need to remind myself that what I write about him is best served as a testimony, rather than delving deeply into the whys and wherefores of our differences.

When I was lost, with no cross-addictions I could turn to, all I could do was stare into the limitless abyss of an untended spiritual life—that's where Scott found me, and he led me through the 12 Steps.

I started working the steps at the tail end of my stay in the Homes of Compassion apartment, which Drug Court perceived as a risky place for me to stay. Unlike purpose-built recovery residences, it didn't offer a built-in recovery community to provide 24-hour external accountability. I didn't want to move…again. I was just getting settled, and I was glad to be away from a house filled with sober dudes complaining about someone stealing their food. But Drug Court insisted that I move to an honest-to-goodness recovery house.

The instability that permeated my life had worn me down. During our most recent counseling session, Bruce told me that I was experiencing "anhedonia," the inability to feel pleasure. It's a post-acute withdrawal symptom (PAWS) common amongst newly recovering drug addicts. I'd been clean from street drugs for almost a year and a half by then, so I didn't expect to be experiencing PAWS with such intensity. Then again, I had found ways to substitute meth-manufactured dopamine hits by snorting my Wellbutrin prescription ever since I got "clean," as well as continuing to engage in parts of The Life. I hadn't given my brain the requisite 18 months necessary to heal properly.

I was finally healing, which proved to be a complicated process. Everything in the material world seemed pointless and useless. The survival mechanisms I'd developed over my whole life to distract me were no longer available—illicit drugs, prescription abuse, codependent relationships, sex addiction, gambling, even pornography. And not just because I'd promised Drug Court that I wouldn't engage in addictive behavior. More importantly, I'd promised myself.

The thought of calling a list of Oxford Houses, asking whether there were vacancies, setting up interviews, and then doing the actual interviews made me want to vomit and hide.

I called my HEN case manager to ask for help with my predicament—within a day, she had reserved a private room in an Eagles Wings recovery house in Port Orchard. That's where I would spend the summer treating my stepwork like a job.

My goal was to finish the long version of the Step Working Guide—all 69 questions—before I restarted the substance use disorder professional program at Olympic College in the fall. I would write 91 pages over four months. Every week, I would drive to Scott's house to review the step I had completed. Sponsors are supposed to sit through an entire reading of a sponsee's step work, but Scott's approach was to make sure that the sponsee in question had written more than a paragraph on the subject, as most people don't want to work that hard on anything at that juncture in their recovery, nor look deeply inward to face their demons. I would write multiple pages per step, so Scott would habitually stop me after one page and call it good.

At the time, I was relieved that I wasn't forced to read aloud all of my prosaic secrets.

Step Three is where most people stop, so when I completed it, I was roaring to beat all of those weak-ass people who had amassed more clean time but couldn't muster the courage to get past Step Three.

Step Four requires "a searching and fearless moral inventory of ourselves," meaning you've got to write down every person you've harmed in your addiction and explain how you did it. Thus far, I had been averaging about 20 hours per week on step work, but Step Four required roughly 40 hours to complete within a week. I did it.

But Scott and Bruce conspired to slow me down—they created extra work for me to complete before I could move on to the next step.

Throughout the entire step-working process, I held onto a lingering doubt that I wrote about in an answer to one of the Step One sub-questions—the thing I feared most about working the steps was that the process might not work, that I'd be wasting my time, that the promised spiritual awakening wouldn't happen. Then I'd have to turn to drugs again.

To my relief (and surprise), my spiritual awakening occurred as I completed Step Eight, which entails making an actual list of all the persons (and entities) I had harmed and becoming willing to make amends to them all. I was lying in bed, obsessing over the amends letters that I would write in Step Nine, as sometimes meeting people and entities in person or even contacting them could injure them or others. In that moment, I gained empathy for the faceless institutions that I had once viewed as both creators and oppressors of the needy, justifying my narcissistic actions. There were real people there, with real faces. would need to make amends to them as well.

Around the same time, I saw Charlotte's post on Facebook—a cry of grief for Ava, who had suddenly died. I messaged Charlotte immediately. Ava had crashed her car about one-quarter mile from her parents' mobile home park; the car had hit an electrical pole, rolled in such a way that the power lines wrapped around her car and electrified it, which endangered the lives of the first responders. Ava died screaming for help while the first responders were forced to wait for the power to be shut off.

Almost a year after this news, I was in my final quarter of the SUDP certificate program, doing my practicum at West Sound Treatment Center in Bremerton. I was observing an outpatient group session as part of my training, where one of the participants recognized me—she was a call girl who had known Ava well and had been competitive with her; she and I had only interacted over Messenger, never having met in person; while I was on the streets, she and I kept trying to make plans to hook up, but she was stuck in Kitsap County and I was gallivanting around the Highway, so coordinating a meeting proved unsuccessful, as one of us would have needed to make the effort to travel cross-county without a car; now in recovery, we had separately found our way to the same treatment facility as client and provider-trainee; she asked me whether I knew that Ava was pregnant when she died. I didn't know.

The first time I shed tears for Ava's was after writing about her in this book. I could sense her presence as I revisited the Messenger thread between us for the first time since she died. It wasn't that I'd been avoiding the emotions. Instead, I had already made my amends to her—the first time was premature, when I had thought that doing the MRT steps prepared me for making amends; the second time was when I did Step Four, writing explicitly and accurately about how I had injured her with my behavior. Charlotte didn't get that chance.

I would see Charlotte again when she arrived at the detox department of the inpatient treatment facility at which I would work after graduating from the SUDP program. She still hadn't gotten over Ava's death.

Working the steps gave me the clarity to accept that death happens to us all; it's just that none of us knows when it will happen. All we can do is make our amends to people before their day comes.

Chapter 10

Phase IV

I need a code to live by—something that tells me how to act in any given context.

This is true for everyone. But for people like me, who may have been given mixed signals about following universal codes (e.g., the Ten Commandments) but then were left to raise themselves or be raised by siblings without the caring reinforcement from emotionally stable and available caregivers required for such codes to become internalized as a moral compass, then people like me find external codes on our own. Growing up, I adopted the overarching code of conduct stemming from America's dog-eat-dog brand of capitalism prevalent in the Madonna-material-girl 1980s: The Ends Justify the Means. Whatever it took to reach my goals, especially manipulation to get my way, was acceptable—in fact, it was commendable as long as the goal was attained. The latter aspect is key to attributing a sense of civility to the potential meanness of the means—attainment of the goal meant that whatever I had to do was justified, but missing the goal untethered any unscrupulous acts perpetrated during the process from possible excuse.

This is why I took so easily to the code of Honor Amongst Thieves—I could be both civilized and a thief.

During my first class in the SUDP certificate program, I was introduced to the National Association of Alcohol and Drug Addiction Counselors (NAADAC) Code of Ethics. Borrowing from established codes of ethics from myriad adjacent helping professions, it states the values of the addiction profession, governing the conduct of NAADAC and its members, while providing a guide for making ethical clinical decisions.

Working the 12 Steps switched on a light in me, but I needed a more concrete code to live by, and the NAADAC Code of Ethics gave me a beneficial code that could replace my old street code.

I bought in right then and there.

Looking back, I now see that this was the pivotal moment in my journey when I decided to remake myself. Different from the point of no return represented by the Determination in Port Angeles, which signified my decision to turn the proverbial corner and take action; different from 12-Step work because, although there was action involved, everything I had written amounted to a plan. A values-driven professional code of ethics told me how to conduct myself as I took action.

When I initially applied to Olympic College at the beginning of the year, I wanted to transfer the relevant credits from the University of Washington bachelor's degree I earned a lifetime ago.

I requested my transcript, and reading it was like opening a time capsule. I always thought my GPA was a 3.0, but I discovered it was actually a 2.95. What the hell? I felt like a remedial student. I poured over the grades for each class—every one of my English courses, which was my major, had a grade of 3.5 or above. But then there was that 8:30 am calculus class during my first quarter: 2.0—that was my 18-year-old self convincing himself that he had the discipline to smoke weed, get drunk, and make it on time to campus from his parents' house across the Evergreen Point Bridge.

Then there were all the 0.0's from the classes that I just stopped attending during my sophomore year—I was seeing a woman who worked at Boeing as a composite parts assembler; she told me I could make good money doing the same job on the graveyard shift, and I convinced myself that I could continue attending classes in the day. We broke up soon after, so I moved into an apartment on Lake Union, where I earned more money than I had ever made in my life, and spent it mainly on going out to bars and clubs.

I finally buckled down in my junior year, though it took me five years to graduate.

All I had to do was drop those unattended classes to maintain a decent grade point, but that would have meant taking responsibility and confronting the registrar five times—I couldn't stand the thought of being judged.

This time around in my educational pursuits, I would heed the words of my parents from my first time in college and treat school like a part-time job—20 hours per week devoted to homework on top of attending classes. I leaned on my writing background to achieve a 100% score on every essay, leveraging the concept of my social service startup as the thesis for most of them. I arrived early and attended nearly every class, with Drug Court commitments being the only reason I ever missed a class (graduating from Drug Court was the legal and ethical priority).

I graduated from the SUDP certificate program in four quarters with a 3.92 GPA, with missed classes the only blemishes.

My clinical studies in how the addict brain works—the effects of psychoactive substances on the natural equilibrium of neurotransmitters, genetic and environmental causes of substance use disorders, and addiction treatment modalities like CBT (cognitive behavioral therapy), made me curious about my inner workings. As I denied myself access to behaviors that masked my internal experiences from my consciousness, the only path to a higher state (of being) was inner healing.

As if on cue from the universe, my younger sister, Maridelle, texted me a podcast from Tara Brach—a renowned western teacher of Buddhist meditation, emotional healing, spiritual awakening, and a clinical psychologist to boot—when I had just begun my search for ways to fill the gaping void inside me that didn't entail consumption of drugs, food, other people, addictive activities, or yet another 12 Step meeting in which everyone would complain about their predicament and then going outside to vape.

The podcast that hooked me was Ms. Brach's lesson on the fearless heart. Suppressing fear is an avoidance strategy that not only doesn't make it go away, but worse yet, increases it. Rather, a fearless heart is created by confronting fear through Ms. Brach's acronym strategy called RAIN: Recognize, Allow, Investigate, and Nurture. It sounds counterintuitive, but the approach captures an age-old teaching in eastern traditions wherein some Buddhist temples require passage through an entrance rendered with sculptures of monstrous deities, as well as ancient Christian texts, such as Dante's Inferno in which Virgil the protagonist confronts the Devil ensconced in ice at the deepest and final level of Hell, with the only way out over the Devil's back, and Purgatory and Heaven await on the other side.

In this pivotal lesson, Ms. Brach taught me that unconfronted fears become inner demons, which, when recognized, allowed, investigated, and counterintuitively nurtured, can revert to "daemons"—the Greek word from which "demon" originates, but which means a divine spirit or power.

My descent into full-time criminal homelessness, which was a way of running away from my unmanageable double life, and consequent participation in Drug Court, was a two-year process of recognizing the existence of my demons. My clinical and ethical studies into the addict brain were my investigation into the trauma responses that I (and most of society) judged as demonic behavior, while the parallel exploration into meditation theory (not so much practice—I still find it challenging to sit and stay for very long) was my way of nurturing the fear that, mistreated, had grown into demons, finally developing the insight to recognize them as guiding spirits.

Only in hindsight can I see that everything I was studying during that year-long season of planting and tending my garden, including the research into nonprofit corporate structures and developing a 501(c)(3) that I did in my spare time, was guided by the ancient aphorism that

God, the universe, and everything will only answer your prayers when you are ready. I was preparing myself to receive the gift of my vision—an organization that would serve the street folks I had left behind, and me, into my old age.

* * *

"I hope I get this new job. I think more money will solve my problems." Dennis sat down with a second helping from the Chinese buffet, where we met for dinner.

My younger brother had driven his Porsche Panamera (his dream car) all the way from his downtown Seattle condominium to attend an NA meeting for the first time at my home group in Port Orchard. His eyes looked artificially bright, but the bags underneath them exposed a weariness. He would tell me later, after he had made his Determination, that during this fateful dinner, he was still reeling from a coke jag the night before and microdosing acid that morning.

I had witnessed his sheen, which I had been envious of when we reconnected over dinner in South Lake Union, had rapidly tarnished since I last saw him in person at the Father's Day get-together Maridelle had hosted the previous summer. There, he announced to everyone, his head lowered in shame, that he had rejoined Gamblers Anonymous because he had recently gambled away $5000—a confession that excluded the amount of money he had lost well before the duration of whatever he defined as "recent."

I was neck-deep in Step work at the time, so although I was itching to sermonize on what I suspected was the true cause of his gambling—namely, his drug addiction—I surprised myself by refraining. Instead, I put an affectionate hand on his shoulder. Over the ensuing months, I would randomly call to check on him and even tried to set up a weekly call, but he was difficult to pin down. When we did talk on the phone, he sounded like a scattered mess, his focus and any meaningful conversation just as tricky to pin down.

After completing a full round of the NA 12 Steps and almost three months into my clinical studies, I finally felt comfortable enough to confront Dennis about what I suspected was the deeper cause of his suffering. He was surprisingly receptive. And like a true drug addict steered toward recovery without the external forces of the justice system, he arrived at his first substance-related 12-Step meeting high.

"Bro. You already make good money. If you can't manage your money now, how can you manage more money?" My question was rich, coming from an absent older brother who had introduced his younger brother to street drugs, while modeling financial irresponsibility throughout our whole lives.

It wasn't until Dennis called me to confess that he had relapsed—not on drugs but gambling—that he was ready to make the Determination. At the time, I was studying the Three Stages of Relapse—emotional relapse (involving vulnerability to and discomfort with a situation that requires as yet undeveloped coping skills), mental relapse (thoughts and cravings for the substance or behavior, including planning the relapse), and physical relapse (committing the actual deed)—and Dennis served as a real-world exercise for me to try out, and hopefully help.

"I feel like I needed to gamble, like, one last time. I just had to get it out of my system. I'm good now." Dennis inadvertently exhaled smoke into the phone.

"That's not how it works. There are three stages of relapse. The first one is emotional. Did something happen that you couldn't deal with?"

"Not really. I mean, I don't know," Dennis hedged. Then, he opened up. "Um, I didn't tell you, but I didn't get the job. Man, that would've taken care of all of my debt. Well, most of it. I think."

"That's what caused your emotional relapse," I was surprised that the trigger was so simple. "Did you start bargaining with yourself about gambling?"

"Totally. I thought since my real problem is my drug addiction, I could go to my old poker night, and it'd be okay as long as I wasn't high." Dennis exhaled so loudly that I could almost taste the smoke.

"Whoa. I was about to ask if you'd planned it. That's a tell-tale sign of the mental relapse. When you went to your poker night, that's the physical relapse." Everything played out in textbook fashion.

"That's crazy. Um, so there's another thing I didn't tell you. I contacted a bankruptcy lawyer."

And there it was: Rock Bottom.

As Dennis entered the most difficult time of recovery—the honest-to-goodness early stage—in parallel, I was absorbing more and more clinical information and trying it all out on him. We would talk on the phone most days, during which I would provide newly learned clinical knowledge along with lived experience—naming the condition and knowing that his experiences were not exclusive to him helped him accept what he was going through.

"I'm so depressed. I can't think of anything that would make me happy." (That's anhedonia.)

"Will I ever start feeling better?" (It takes three months for the brain of a stimulant user to regain equilibrium.)

"Is there anything I can take to make me feel better?" (Cokeheads and meth-heads aren't as lucky as junkies when it comes to MAT, medication assisted treatment; there isn't anything that can pharmaceutically ease the cravings of a stimulant high like Suboxone can for opioid users—except Adderall, which is an actual amphetamine and creates dependence—but ask your doctor for Wellbutrin, which sort of helps…just keep it away from me when I come to visit.)

"I had a dream last night that I relapsed on coke. It was so real. I even feel guilty about it." (That's PAWS—post acute withdrawal symptoms—unlike acute withdrawal, which is the physical withdrawal symptoms when you stop taking drugs, PAWS are primarily psychological and emotional symptoms that can last for up to two years; it's normal.)

Drug Court didn't think twice when I asked to spend the night at Dennis' place regularly so that I could keep an eye on him and attend 12-Step meetings on his side of the Puget Sound. He quickly got himself a home group and a sponsor, who guided him through a complete round of the Steps.

To this day, Dennis attends more meetings than I do. He is fully ensconced in multiple 12 Step fellowships and is pursuing a master's degree in divinity—Christianity is his spiritual gig in recovery, and I'm proud to say that he's not a dick about it either.

He ain't heavy. He's my brother.

***

If I had had the foresight to develop a training course that would give me frontline experience in the myriad business models within the recovery residence landscape in order to leverage this educational survey to inform the operating model for my eventual social service agency, I could not have done any better than the mostly unplanned and decidedly mercurial series of moves that happened after I got kicked out of my one and only Oxford House.

After getting kicked out of the Hewitt Oxford House when Drug Court finally caught me red-handed (or, in my case, nose-powdered) and then spending six weeks at an inpatient facility, the ABHS case manager secured a spot for me in a Homes of Compassion.

I ended up in one of their "next step" homes for people in stable recovery who have emotionally graduated from the community-policing of an Oxford House but either don't yet have the resources to afford their own place, or haven't coupled up to share the costs of, say, a two-bedroom apartment with a significant other. As much as I rebelled against Drug Court's assessment that I was not ready for a less structured environment, being recently released from inpatient treatment made me de facto emotionally unready.

Since I didn't have the emotional energy to deal with looking for and interviewing with another Oxford House, I cried to my HEN case manager about my predicament and got placed in an Eagles Wings—another nonprofit addressing homelessness.

I was supposed to move into a brand-new Eagles Wings in Gorst, a little town between Bremerton and Port Orchard. I would have been the first tenant in the new house, which felt good because it meant I could now be trusted to be a pillar of a new tiny recovery community. But the opening of the new house kept getting delayed. As the start of my second college career approached, I needed to find a spot closer to Olympic College—the Eagles Wings Clevenger House, where I had spent the summer working the Steps, was deep in the outskirts of Port Orchard, making a potential commute to the Bremerton campus economically impractical for someone subsisting on school loans and scholarships.

The Kitsap County Drug Court Alumni Association, a small group of Drug Court graduates that operates a nonprofit organization comprised solely of people who have remained in recovery and volunteered their services for small community projects, had been planning to open their recovery residence for current Drug Court participants. As my time at the Clevinger House dragged on, the opening of the Alumni House was suddenly just a couple of months away.

Scott informed me that he was going to be the house manager, so I devised a business and operating model that would make the Alumni House a rousing success. I had it all figured out, and I believed that my two years of surveying different recovery residence models, completing the 12 Steps, and my formidable business background from my past life had endowed me with more wherewithal than anyone else involved.

This was my attitude when I left Eagles Wings behind and moved into the Alumni House.

When Scott didn't become the house manager, I was as resentful as he was at the injustice of it all—I allowed my blind faith in my recovery sponsor and newly minted business co-founder to judge the other house managers as unworthy of their posts. Making matters worse, I was in my first quarter in the SUDP certificate program, developing the requisite fervor to my newly adopted code of ethics as that of a religious acolyte, while having picked up just enough clinical knowledge to become as dangerous as a sick person Googling their symptoms.

These factors coalesced into dogmatic assessments of anything that the house managers might be doing that didn't fit into my rigid definitions. I had no consideration for the trials and mistakes of well-meaning human beings trying their very best to start up an enterprise built to support self-centered and unstable people new in recovery and involved in the justice system.

My self-imposed isolation—talking with no one except for Scott about my issues with the house managers—created an environment so oppressive that I convinced myself that I didn't feel safe. I wanted out of that place within three months. It was the final two weeks of the year, and the entire Drug Court team was on holiday. However, Samantha, the treatment court manager, had become a supportive advisor, so she scheduled a Zoom call to discuss my predicament.

At the beginning of our business partnership, Scott talked about our concept to whomever would listen within his vast community network, getting our initial business plan into the hands of Drug Court-associated folks. Eventually, the document landed in Samantha's inbox. She loved it and became our strategic advisor; we became her protégés.

Scott and I attended meetings with Samantha, during which she would advise us on whom to contact to drum up support for our initiative. I would find out later, during my Drug Court graduation panel—where soon-to-be graduates sit in front of the entire Drug Court team to receive final assessments before graduation ceremonies—that Samantha didn't trust me for the first 16 months of my program participation. She could tell I was up to no good. But when she read the Drug Court amends letter I had mailed to Laurel, who worked for Samantha, she allowed herself to start trusting me. By the time of our emergency Zoom call, Samantha knew that an integral part of our fledgling business's operations plan entailed temporarily housing our first clients in motel rooms, with me living amongst them as an onsite manager. This plan was my way of living The Life without having to fall back into the tawdriness of it all.

"You want to move into a motel?" Samantha was skeptical.

"You know it's part of my vision. This is the perfect opportunity for me to test things out."

"Which motel are you thinking?"

"The one where HEN put me up before I went to inpatient. I still need to ask them, though."

"Well, you're stabilized now. You've been performing well since entering Phase 4. But we have to get Judge H's permission, and I'm not certain of that," Samantha hedged.

"I know. But one way or another, I have to get out of here."

Within a couple of days, I got the go-ahead from Samantha.

I asked my HEN case manager if my rental assistance could be applied towards a motel room, adding that Drug Court had already permitted the move. My case manager said she had to talk with Skye, who was the second person to whom I had emailed the most recent version of my business plan—I kept her continually apprised of the progress of my project, so she already knew of my plans to live in a motel room amongst my first clients.

The next day, my HEN case manager told me the good news: "Skye said you get three months, and then we have to figure out other arrangements."

* * *

It was one of my worst decisions ever.

In terms of discovering that living in a motel room was NOT what I wanted to do ever again, then this move turned out to be one of my best ever decisions. But the experience absolutely sucked.

I thought I knew exactly what I was getting into, and for the most part, I did. I had already stayed at that exact property less than a year before;

I had frequented such establishments while I was on the streets, always looking forward to and appreciating the warmth and protection that such accommodations provided to my erstwhile homeless existence, regardless of the enduringly unkempt and rundown nature of every motel catering to the liminally housed.

During my two years of living in recovery residences, all I ever noticed was the incivility of the environment—a bunch of emotionally underdeveloped grown men living obnoxiously out loud—listening to music, watching television, playing on their phones, even snoring—leaving dishes in the sink, and generally behaving like 200-lbs 12-year-olds with absent parents. I romanticized that the domiciles of early recovery weren't much different from the motel existence that I had left behind—the people were the same, the only difference being active drug taking on one side and abstinence on the other.

But I wasn't aware of the change in my perceptions and expectations. I didn't anticipate the level of repugnance I would experience daily, and the effects on my mental health. I didn't expect the level of resentment toward the owners and management for the deliberate squalor of the living conditions, all in the name of maintaining profit margins. The constant repression invoked a decision to buy the property one day and turn it into a recovery residence, providing amenities designed to instill self-respect in the tenants, while generating sustainable profits.

During my first few days, I thought that I had lucked out being placed on the grassy knoll, facing a long, fenced lawn away from the courtyard of constantly rotating cars and loud-mouthed guests high as kites. The majority of the tenants on lowest level were permanent, to the extent that one could call liminal housing as such, having lived there for months or years. The door to my room was rotting and didn't fit snugly in the doorway, exposing a little gap. For my own hygiene, I needed to replace the nasty shower curtain with a new one that I bought myself, along with a waterproof mattress cover to protect myself from the stains on the mattress.

But it was relatively quiet and all mine.

It wasn't until my first weekend that I noticed my new living situation's fatal flaw. The room next to me was vacant, meaning guests would stay there temporarily, which meant they wouldn't uphold the same decorum as the permanent residents. The first such visitors that I encountered were loudly hanging outside their door to smoke, which sounded as clear as an open door through the crack in my door seal.

The next round of vagabonds would talk excitedly in their room, which, through the thin walls, allowed me to eavesdrop on their conversations unwillingly. I could usually drown out most of the unwelcome voices by turning up the television volume. But at night, when trying to get to bed at a decent hour to make it to college in the morning, I had no such recourse, so I just fumed myself to sleep, which didn't work, which meant I attended my morning class bleary-eyed and brimming with resentment.

What should have been the last straw occurred during the third month of my stay. A Filipino guy around my age and his white girlfriend moved in for over a week. I saw him one day when he was outside talking and gesticulating to one of his cronies, as I was returning to my little shanty. I could tell he was Filipino a few nights before that incident—through the walls, I heard his conversation with his mother on FaceTime; she was speaking in a sad and guilt-inducing tone with an unmistakably Filipino accent, whimpering every so often, while he yelled and screamed at her like a pouty little boy. As I rolled around in bed, trying desperately to meditate the noxious energy away, images of me throwing an adult tantrum down the phone to my mother, who had just done something codependent that she thought was helpful but that I perceived as having ruined my life.

This scene played out over the thin walls every other night. During off nights, I could hear him reprimanding his girlfriend for some perceived disloyalty—he played the same critical victim role with each of the women in his life, and they played their own reciprocal victim role, rotating places every other night. The bass in his low voice was like mine, cutting through the walls like a subwoofer and holding up another mirror into which I was forced to gaze.

I pounded on the wall when I couldn't take it anymore. The noise would stop...for a while...then start up again.

I complained about them to management, who advised me to call the cops (this is the typical response of proprietors of rundown, seedy motels). It was the middle of the night, and I didn't want to deal with being the witness, so the next day, I waited for them to get loud again. Eventually, they got loud, so I called the police to complain about a domestic violence situation. A female police officer showed up fairly quickly, but then all I could overhear were apologies to the police officer and laughter afterwards. Those motherfuckers were all in on it and mocking me.

Then, on one beautiful spring day in March, everything was quiet—they had moved on. But real peace never returned, as the hypervigilance I had worked so hard to mitigate through recovery reemerged, listening for the tell-tale sounds of some new potential noise perpetrator moving in next door.

As I wondered how I would survive another toxic neighbor, and if not, what might my options be for retaining my own space on a HEN budget, I received a letter from DSHS (Department of Social and Health Services) reminding me that it was time for my annual reassessment for the ABD (Aged, Blind, and Disabled) benefit. I started receiving this paltry cash benefit after my COVID-era unemployment benefits ended. as substance use and co-occurring disorders were deemed benefit-worthy disabilities.

As helpful as the monthly stipend was, the automatic eligibility for HEN rental assistance was the most valuable benefit, so I wanted to keep it. The DSHS staff psychologist called me on the scheduled day and time, and asked me the requisite mental health screening questions, which I would study in the Abnormal Psychology course that I would take during summer quarter. Had I been educated on the goal of the mental health screening to assess whether I was still in crisis, then I would have known that I shouldn't have tried to pass it. But pass it I did—with flying colors—and assessed as no longer in crisis.

Now, I was ineligible for ABD benefits, including HEN rental assistance. The three months that HEN allowed me to experiment with living in a motel coincided with the abrupt end of receiving the benefits altogether.

"I want to stay here. So, I need to go to KCR and see if I can get rental assistance from them," I told Mrs. Carr. When Laurel decided that five years of working for Drug Court was enough and quit, Mrs. Carr took over part of her caseload, which included me.

"You are less than two months from graduating from Drug Court. You should not be on rental assistance anymore. I want you to create a budget that includes paying your own rent in a recovery house. From what you've been telling me about that place, you need to move from there, anyway." Mrs. Carr demanded discipline; it was her way of caring.

"Yeah, I know."

"Email your budget to me by tomorrow."

"Tomorrow?"

"Yes. You can do it," she encouraged.

I did it.

I hadn't created a budget in years, maybe a decade. I stopped trying to control my money when I stopped paying bills altogether. But I saw that the income from my student loans and scholarships would allow me to cover rent in a recovery residence.

The previous week, I had parked my car at the Kitsap Recovery Center outpatient facility to attend my monthly group session. As I closed the car door, I saw another car stop in the middle of the road and heard my name called. It was two of my ex-housemates from the Eagles Wings Clevenger House. They were managing a new recovery residence literally a block away. After my talk with Mrs. Carr, I called them to see if they had a room available.

I moved into Joe Mama's House the following week. There, I would get to know the owner, Ty, who moved his family out of the two houses nestled in the same property to create a tribute to his fallen brother, Joe, who had died of an opioid overdose and was known as Joe Mama on the streets.

The summer after graduating from Drug Court, I was halfway through the arduous process of building my nascent organization's Board of Directors. My biggest get, which marked the moment when things started falling into place, was Mirelle, the faculty head overseeing my SUDP certificate program, agreeing to take on the role of president. I recognized this was a significant risk for her—I was merely on the cusp of graduation and would be an unknown in a field filled with ethical landmines. But she believed in her students and wanted to show that belief on a practical and tangible level.

I also wanted a business leader to provide balance to the community leaders who eventually would make up the majority of the Board. But none of the corporate leaders in my LinkedIn network felt they would make a good fit. Ty was one of the top salespeople in Ford's national network of franchises, a self-made man who pulled himself up from substance use and prison. He would become the third and final original Board member.

Mrs. Carr's demand-encouragement scheduled that divine appointment.

* * *

Drug Court graduation loomed.

Luckily, I was the very first Joemama's house resident (outside of the house managers), so I got my own room for a while. This was a good thing, as the stress of graduation made me unfit to room with anyone.

When I was new to Drug Court, I would scoff at the Phase 4 folks attending group sessions once a month, ungrateful bastards who had it so easy yet continued to complain about the stress of their upcoming graduation. They worried incessantly about potentially missing obligations, mental health appointments, and especially random urinalyses. I didn't buy any of it. On the precipice of my own graduation, I knew exactly what they meant. Any slip-up would result in having to redo Phase 4, all six months of it.

But I made it.

The location of Joemama's House—one block from my outpatient facility (where I was required to attend monthly group sessions), two blocks from my NA home group meeting (where I was required to attend meetings three times per week), and four blocks from the Kitsap County Superior Courthouse (where I was required to appear in court once per month)—supported my cause.

My one-year recovery birthday landed four days before Drug Court graduation ceremonies, and I had the most vivid using dream that I ever had during recovery. In the dream, I was lamenting the loss of my clean date, being forced to redo all of Phase 4, and most of all, losing the faith and trust of the people who had thrown their support behind me. In a split second of weakness, I lost everything I'd worked for the past 27 months. When I woke up and found myself in the living room (having moved there in the middle of the night to get away from the new guy, whose snoring blasted through the thin curtains separating the upstairs rooms), I was so relieved that I cried (a little bit).

At every Drug Court graduation ceremony, the graduates are seated at a long table where the County Commissioners typically preside. Seating arrangements are ordered based on increasingly awful mugshots, from least to worst—I was second to last. When my name was finally called, I walked down the stage stairs and took my place next to Judge H, who said some fair and tender things about me. Then, Mrs. Carr said a few words, but since her case management duties encompassed only the final months of my tenure, she quickly handed the lectern over to Bruce, who said some very cool things about me. Finally, he handed the lectern over to a surprise speaker on my behalf, Carol, which warmed my heart.

As with every graduate, my last booking photo—the very same one that kicks off this memoir—was projected onto a large screen for the entire audience to witness, portraying how far I'd come.

Chapter 11

Launch

By and For Organizations are operated by and for the communities they serve. Their mission is to serve the community from which they came and in which they continue to live, with their organization substantially directed and controlled by members from the population they serve. At the core of their programs, these organizations represent the central cultural values of their community and target population.

It is a noble aspiration and makes practical sense—who better to provide needed services to the needy in the community than the people with lived experience, who have waded through the muck of an inequitable society, found the way to navigate through the administrative labyrinth of government benefits, developed the courage and resilience to remake themselves in the face of unforgiving segments of society, found the support of a likeminded community, and against all odds, came out the other side with a burning desire to reach back into the pit from whence they came and pull up others mired in similar predicaments.

The reality in the recovery community is that it is full of the most imperfect people who have cultivated a self-centeredness that even in recovery continues to hover at the border of pathology, retaining at some level the lifetime habit of covering up their imperfections to others and denying their imperfections to themselves. Someone in recovery can be as abstinent as a monk or nun, but the spectrum of pathological denial on one end and self-awareness on the other doesn't always coincide with their clean and sober time.

When dealing with populations coming straight out of prisons, jails, intensive inpatient facilities, or right out of an encampment, self-awareness—being completely honest with yourself about your strengths and weaknesses, what triggers your emotions, the ability to name your emotions, allowing them to exist, letting them pass, and then knowing whether you need counsel to make the next right move—is the most essential trait in providing ethical support to vulnerable populations. But years of abstinence are no guarantee.

The noble and practical construct of the by-and-for organization most often falls apart, or at least is ethically stretched, when addiction professionals must provide services to someone with whom they had a previous relationship. There's no way to avoid being thrust into a situation where you are duty-bound to serve someone with whom you used to get high.

A few months into my job at Kitsap Recovery Center (KRC) inpatient facility in Port Orchard, this happened to me.

After graduating from the SUDP certificate program, I sought a part-time job in the addiction field to continue allocating time to launching my startup. I asked Carol and Bruce to put in a good word for me at KRC's inpatient facility. Following a COVID outbreak and a subsequent two-week shutdown, HR finally called me for an interview. There, I told them how I had been waiting in my car parked in front of the Kitsap County Human Resources building, which was across the street from the Superior Courthouse, which in turn was situated in front of the county jail, from which I had been released almost three years from the date of the interview. Who knew I would end up back in that same area, trying to get a job to help people with the same outlook I had almost three years ago—lost and angry at the world.

I got the job and started on the graveyard shift.

Living in transitional housing, where the majority of the dudes are in early recovery, sucks for graveyard work. They're loud, running up and down the wooden staircase or watching TV with the sound turned up—

my room was sandwiched between the stairs and the living room. So, I had to train and bribe my housemates—I bought headphones for the guys who didn't own a pair and purchased a Bluetooth receiver for the dumb TV so that the guys could watch and listen using their headphones while I tried to get some sleep during the day. But the setup wasn't foolproof. I'd invariably wake up at 10 pm pissed off at everyone.

Eventually, newly released inpatients from KRC started trickling in as residents, creating an ethical dilemma of dual relationships—the NAADAC code of ethics states that "addiction professionals shall make every effort to avoid multiple relationships with a client," and living in the same recovery house with a previous client counts. The situation forced me to advise Ty that I'd have to start planning my move.

Around the same time, one of the treatment aides had a nervous breakdown and went on disability leave. The addiction treatment profession is notorious for being overworked, underpaid, and emotionally draining. With staffing already at a skeleton level, this employee's absence meant overtime for everyone. When I started the job, I set my newfound boundaries and was adamant that I wouldn't work overtime, a position I'd successfully maintained until the nervous breakdown incident. But it was time for everyone to pull together. With my usual interrupted sleep and now forced to wake up earlier to log 12-hour shifts, I was continuously spent.

Even with all the undue pressure, a part of me looked forward to going to work because Charlotte was there as a patient.

It had been nearly two weeks since I saw her name on the whiteboard in the detox station. The whiteboard contains an ever-changing list of detox patients, coming and going every 3-5 days. To be clear, there had been a handful of times when someone with whom I'd had a previous relationship came through, but until I saw Charlotte's name on the patient list, they were only people I had met while in recovery who had relapsed.

When I shuffled into the detox station the night Charlotte had arrived, still wiping sleep from eyes, I scanned the whiteboard to see the number of patients who would be in my charge—checking on them every 20 minutes to deter potential suicides, taking their vital signs every three hours to monitor their health during detoxification, sending unstable patients to the emergency room, bringing snacks to patients whose come-downs activated their appetites, performing intakes on new patients (the most emotionally demanding task and the one I looked forward to the least), dispensing prescription medications in the morning, and helping the kitchen staff prepare the patients' breakfast. When I saw Charlotte's name on the whiteboard, I knew it was her—she was the only woman with that name in the drug circles around Kitsap.

She arrived at the behest of Behavioral Health Court, a diversion program similar to Drug Court but at the municipal level, targeting justice-involved people with more serious co-occurring disorders than Drug Court participants usually present. With Charlotte's horrendous childhood and the institutional abuse that she experienced in adulthood, the courts saw that throwing her back in prison for whatever crime she committed this time around would perpetuate the abuse cycle.

Watching Charlotte's withdrawals from smoking dozens of fentanyl pills daily was hard for me. She was required to metabolize the massive amounts of fentanyl coursing through her before starting her methadone course, a medication-assisted therapy she chose over Suboxone because she thought it was stronger and would give her a better chance at remaining abstinent. When Charlotte was finally ready to start her methadone course, I was so grateful (and relieved) to be in the professional position to dispense her doses. After a longer-than-usual stay in the detox department, she was moved over to the inpatient side, where she would remain for another 28 days.

Med call was the morning shift's task, so Charlotte's move to the inpatient side took the responsibility (and, if I'm sincere, enjoyment) of dispensing her dose from me.

But when I was forced to come into work four hours earlier, it coincided with the task of evening med call. I would get the chance to give Charlotte her drugs.

She was the last person in line for meds that night. Her list of medications was thankfully short, so I gave her the pills on her list first.

"I have a confession to make. Giving you your drugs satisfies the inner drug dealer in me."

Charlotte chuckled and smiled. After writing my initials next to the prescription pills that I had dispensed, which is the process of officially recording the medication log, I opened the lock box containing her methadone bottles. All narcotics are secured and tightly controlled. I gave her a bottle, and she happily drank it. I was supposed to have checked the medication log before dispensing her dose, but my sleepy, overworked, and enthusiastic mind told me it was time for her dose.

No, it wasn't.

I checked Charlotte's methadone log—she had already taken her once-a-day dose in the morning. Methadone is not like Suboxone, which can be taken more than once per day.

"Um, you already had your dose today?" I felt sick to my stomach.

"Yeah, but they were talking about increasing my dose anyway."

"I just messed up. I like giving you your drugs way too much. I need to write myself up."

"Will I get in trouble?"

"Not as much as me. You should go back to your room."

I conducted myself at work by the book. Adhering to standard operating procedures was my way of living by a code. Doing so proved to me that I was coming from a place of integrity. The overriding ethical principle by which I interacted with clients was Justice, which I interpreted as no favoritism. This incident was the first time I had addressed Charlotte differently from the other clients, and this single act disintegrated my integrity.

The only way that I could stop the bleeding was to tell on myself. I wrote an incident report...on myself. Then, I texted my manager, Brian, and informed him of what had happened. As I waited for his response like a forlorn lover, checking my phone every minute, I told on myself to my workmates on the group chat. Nearly everyone responded with their own horrifying stories of medication mismanagement—the incident became part of the initiation into the field of intensive inpatient addiction treatment.

None of it made me feel better. Only when Brian called back did my dread begin to lift.

"You messed up. But I appreciate you telling me right away. This is your first offense, and you're doing well, so just make sure someone else is with you when dispensing medication to Charlotte. Put the incident report on my desk."

"Thank you. But for as long as Charlotte is here, I'd rather not dispense any medications to her. I'll get someone else to do it. I enjoy it too much."

Over the next few days, the strangest thing happened—everyone on the team was extra cool, smiling at me more, not just the perfunctory work smile, which is always a little bit forced, but with a sincerity that was plain to see. They trusted me...explicitly.

Charlotte and I steered clear of each other for the remainder of her stay. On the morning of her departure, she made a point to stop by the detox office before I finished my graveyard shift to show me a framed photo of her baby daughter, little Ava.

I haven't heard from Charlotte since.

* * *

It took three months to find a place of my own.

My credit score, which had risen over 100 points over the past two years, still sucked—it had dipped below 500 while I scammed my profile, had my car repossessed, and house foreclosed. All of the forced overtime had the fortunate effect of creating a small deposit fund for an apartment, but none of the traditional leasing companies would give me a chance due to the wake of destruction that was my credit history.

I had no other option but to approach private landlords, come clean, and share my story.

I scanned the Craigslist For Rent listings, stitched together a likely list of candidates, and emailed them this testimony...

Hello-

I'm interested in the apartment you have for rent.

I currently work full-time on the graveyard shift at Kitsap Recovery Center addiction treatment facility in Port Orchard. I'm a graduate of the Kitsap County Drug Court program and in long-term recovery from substance use disorder, as well as a graduate of the Olympic College Substance Use Disorder Professional Certificate program.

I've been living in recovery residences for a few years now and am ready to take the next step. Your apartment, being manageable in size and near my job, seems like the right next step.

However, my credit report has created a barrier during my apartment search. It is part of the wreckage of my past that I am still working on. But as I work through this process, it will not prevent me from paying my rent on time. Please let me know if you can work with this before I submit a rental application.

As a tenant, I would treat your property in the same manner as I conduct myself in every aspect of my life—conscientiously and disciplined, operating on principles and integrity.

Of the six missives, I received two replies, both of which were so supportive of my cause that I was overwhelmed with emotion and cried to myself while everyone in the house slept. I can't find the first response in my old emails—I was this close to closing the deal with the landlord, and the price-to-quality ratio was unheard of, but someone who contacted him before I had appeared decided to take the studio; as a man of his word, the landlord was forced to decline my application.

The second reply was also a decline, but just as encouraging...

Hello,

Thank you for your well-written and thoughtful email. The unit you inquired about has been rented. If something comes up, I can certainly reach out. Keep up the great work, and I hope to have you as a tenant in the future.

Encouragement doesn't pay the bills, though, nor does it land an apartment.

The more my apartment search dragged on, the more critical I became of the guys in the house, for no other reason than that I was stuck with them. I criticized every little thing anyone did. I was hell to live with. I would drive my car down to the waterfront and sit in it for hours, just to escape the house and the powerlessness I felt there.

Then, I had the idea that my non-living wage might make me eligible for subsidized housing—not quite low income, but with a low credit score, which is a form of low income. That was the answer. I found a two-bedroom in a subsidized community in East Bremerton, containing a mix of Section 8 and "mid-income" housing; hence, property management didn't expect the highest credit scores. They did, however, exclude applicants with felony convictions, so Drug Court cleaning my record proved beneficial.

I moved into my new place three years and one-and-a-half months after being released from Kitsap County Jail on personal recognizance for the last time, living in five different recovery residences and a motel over that period, and five years from the advent of my homelessness.

On the first day in my new apartment, after I had built my new bed frame and Scott picked up a sofa for me at Goodwill for $2.50, I sat in the living room, feeling small and overwhelmed. I didn't know what to do with all that space. Over the course of five years, the amount of space that my outer presence occupied had shrunk, and my inner presence had followed suit. It would take months before I furnished the place to a comfortable yet minimalist level, with my inner presence expanding to fill the space in parallel.

***

I must have submitted 15 grant applications over two months. Only one had been awarded for a small sponsorship of the clean and sober softball team I played on. But I had no idea how much rejection after rejection was affecting me until I received a call from the Silverdale Rotary Club. Although they informed me that my application had been declined, they soothed me with words of encouragement, saying that I was doing important work and not to give up. At that moment, all of the stress wound like a coil inside me seemed to spring open, and I broke down in tears. I don't try to dampen my tears anymore. I've been trained to let it all out. So, I did, for about 15 minutes on my living room floor, next to the $2.50 sofa.

About a week later, I saw the request for proposal on the Washington State Department of Commerce site for the Reentry Grant Program, looking for small community-based agencies that did exactly what Homey Corps does.

The grant amount would be substantial enough to support full-time operations and provide me with a salary, albeit slightly lower than my current salary. Filling out the application, I found that I'd been doing this type of work for 20 Years—the components of an institutional grant proposal were no different than the business cases and project plans required to obtain venture capital or corporate resources. Still, I was unsure—and vulnerable from all the recent rejections. To make matters worse, there had been a delay in announcing the award due to an unusually high volume of applications—more competition meant a lower chance of success.

Two months after submitting the application, I woke up at noon to get ready for the swing shift. I had graduated from graveyard and found the schedule suited me naturally. I checked my phone but didn't want to open the email. I was scared that it might be another rejection. My eyes were still blurry from sleep. I couldn't make out the subject line. I just knew it was from the Washington State Department of Commerce.

Finally, I focused my eyes and opened the email…

Greetings:

Appreciate your patience. Please see attached Notice of Apparent Successful Contractors. Congrats!

That was the best high of my life.

Chapter 12

Epilogue

The language used in recovery revolves around love, support, and by definition, accountability. At first, this love language feels foreign and uncomfortable to people like me. But after a while, we become fluent, and then it becomes our native language.

We never let each other forget from whence we all came, and that shared lived experience is what makes us each other's people.

* * *

Ronin, against all odds, was the only guy from the streets with whom I had kept in touch. I initially reached out to him when I launched the first iteration of the Homey Corps website. I wanted to show it off to the smartest of all my street folks, someone who I thought could eventually become a valuable team member.

But, independent to a fault, Ronin was on his own path—meeting a woman who inspired him to get into recovery, and then moving in with her...

MAR 23, 6:18 PM

ME: "I wrote about the time Harry sent you to track me down and you took my backpack. But I'm also going to write about how we kept in touch, and how you got into recovery on your own."

RONIN: "Aww really??? That's cool. I will definitely have to check your book out. Likewise, long way from where we were...it's definitely a struggle to get just a little piece of what I used to have. Things are still a struggle."

ME: "You're building something different than what you had because that was unsustainable."

RONIN: "Damn dude. Just went through our whole history in my head… we were crazy, pissed, outta control, etc…BUT we both kinda found our calling, destiny, or our purpose."

ME: "We're a lot alike. Competitive, even with each other, like the best players on the same team."

* * *

Joey lived in the Hewitt Oxford House with me. We were both in Drug Court.

But being young and full of himself at the time, he got caught up engaging in old behavior, running and gunning, which he recorded on Facebook. Drug Court terminated him, and he was sent to prison, while his girlfriend, Katelyn, was pregnant with their son. Luckily, after two years, Joey was released on DOSA (Drug Offender Sentencing Alternative), a diversion program that provides eligible individuals convicted of drug-related offenses with an opportunity for treatment instead of lengthy incarceration.

Joey and Katelyn are my recovery kids. They check up on me once in a while…

MAR 12, 8:56 PM

ME: "Thanks for getting me out. I'd been isolating a little. It was nice at the NA meeting when Katelyn put Junior on my lap and said, Here, go to grandpa."

JOEY: "Yeah. We miss you, Arnel. It was good to see you bud."

ME: "As for you guys trying to save folks you used to know, remember, you have to maintain strong boundaries when helping people. You don't need to let them stay at your place. Your home is sacred."

JOEY: "I know. I'm not gonna do that one again for sure. At least one of them made it to detox."

ME: "That was your learning experience. I'm proud of what both of you have become. To think that you knocked up Katelyn in the downstairs bathroom no less, before getting terminated. Now look at you. Ha."

JOEY: "Ya, thank you. A lot of time and growing up. And you've come far as well. Don't think I forgot about what you were doing in your hobbit hole at Oxford lol."

* * *

Josh hit a softball straight to me.

A Drug Court graduate years before me, he recently agreed to serve as the new President of the Homey Corps Board of Directors while working full-time with the Poulsbo Police Department while only recently earning a Master of Social Work degree. He also coaches a clean and sober softball team in his spare time.

Josh's team was scrimmaging our team the last weekend before the start of the spring sober softball season. This would be my third year playing in the league, without ever having played a sport with a ball, bat, and glove growing up. As a softball newbie, I was forced to practice humility, discipline, and vulnerability to learn the game.

I was playing left field, the most challenging outfield position, as most hits tend to come that way. Josh's hit kept sailing, and I found myself out of position. I reached for it, but it was just out of reach and glanced off my glove.

Josh legged it out to a double.

"Did you do that because you love me?" Josh beamed from second base.

"No." I pretended to be as mad at Josh as I was at myself.

He wasn't buying it.

*　*　*

I sent the advance review copy of this book to everyone whose real name appears in "Part II: Recovery." One of those people was Arminda, my eldest sister.

While writing the vignette where her family appears, which occurred at the end of my first year on the streets, I remembered fully intending to come clean to them about the sinister trajectory on which my life had careened.

I would be my most humble self (whatever that meant to me at the time).

I would pour out the darkness of my heart so that they might cleanse it.

Apparently, that's not what the high version of me portrayed...

From: Arminda <xxxx@gmail.com>
Sent: Wednesday, September 10, 2025 11:28 PM
To: Arnel Leyva <xxxx@outlook.com>; Nick <xxxxx@gmail.com>
Subject: Re: My Memoir

Dear Brother,

I must admit and apologize that I have not yet finished your book. It has been an arduous endeavor, considering the intimate nature of it. I also don't have the mental, psychological, or emotional bandwidth to tackle much nowadays.

Regardless, I must first and foremost commend your writing. You write well. You always have – except when you get in your own way (I, too, find the em dash useful). You largely avoided that in this book. People and their actions—not your thesaurus—take center stage. Bravo!

Now here comes the but... That was one lifeless, lacking paragraph you gave us—a singularly meaningless interaction that does not deserve mention as-is.

I'd like to tell you what happened at Dick's Drive-In and its ultimate import. I get that you didn't understand or remember what happened because you were so steeped in your addiction, so let me tell you the story.

You approached us with an air of both subterfuge and braggadocio. You boasted of lifting credit card numbers on newly minted credit cards that hadn't been delivered yet, among other illegal activities. "This is the hard core shit I've been up to," you bragged.

You told us, "I'm a criminal." Bob then asked, "But have you actually been convicted?" You said, well no. "Then you're not a criminal," Bob quipped.

That was a joke. But you were so intent on swaggering – and engulfed in addiction – that you didn't get it. After you'd relayed your exploits and where it's taken you, Bob said, "This is the point where you have to give up all your autonomy. If you truly want help, that's what you have to do. Not help your way or on your terms. You must give up the idea that you're in charge."

You asked Bob, "What exactly do you mean by that?"

This floored Nick. He was confused as to what in that plain English was so hard for you to understand. Then again, Nick is Bob's and my son, and he has been inculcated in our philosophy and values. He also has his head squarely on his shoulders. But I digress.

What we did tell you in no uncertain terms was that you must set aside your ego and follow instructions. The addiction is in charge of your physiology and psychology—in that order.

Your agency is in recognizing and acknowledging that and taking the first of the 12 steps.

I also asked you, "What happened to your face? Your jaw? You don't look like yourself." You told me you lost some teeth. I gave you $200 out of sympathy.

Then you gave Nick your cheap Marshall brand headphones, saying, "Sorry this is the best I can do for a Christmas gift (for your godson)."

You were descending to the nadir of your battle with addiction, so you did not recognize that we were a beacon of sanity, having been through it with a loved one. We were showing you a way out. But you weren't ready, and you weren't done going down that hard road.

As for our footnote in your book, on behalf of Nick and myself, you do not have permission to mention us unless you include Bob's punch line and what he told you about recovery. That is the moral of the story, the crux of the interlude at the drive-in.

It is a tribute to Bob and his battle with—and triumph over—alcoholism/addiction. He had over 34 years of happy, painless sobriety.

Sincerely, with Love,

A...

From: Arnel Leyva <xxxx@outlook.com>

Sent: Wednesday, September 11, 2025 10:37 AM

To: Arminda <xxxx@outlook.com>; Nick <xxxxx@gmail.com>

Subject: Re: My Memoir

Thank you for this.

I hadn't remembered any of it. Because of that, I tried to provide a testimony rather than elaborate on fuzziness. The original version I wrote included Bob's line, which is enshrined in my memory, but then I thought that I would come across as bragging.

I was writing that part of the book when Bob was in hospice, and I wasn't sure how to fittingly memorialize him.

Thank you for rebuilding my memory by reliving that traumatic event. Seeing your perspective was a jolt. If you and Nick don't mind, I would like to insert what you've written in my book.

From: Arminda <xxxx@gmail.com>

Sent: Wednesday, September 11, 2025 7:18 PM

To: Arnel Leyva <xxxx@outlook.com>; Nick <xxxxx@gmail.com>

Subject: Re: My Memoir

Yes, you certainly do have my/our permission. The waterworks are flowing as I write this…anything and everything can make me do that these days. I love you, O Brother who art now with Us. I'm so, so glad you're in a much better place now. Take good care.

The End.

The End.

Please leave a review wherever you bought my book—whether you loved it, hated it, or somewhere in between.

Thank you.

www.ingramcontent.com/pod-product-compliance
Lightning Source LLC
Chambersburg PA
CBHW011407070526
44586CB00022B/2590